EDIFICATION

The Ray S. Anderson Collection

Ray Sherman Anderson (1925–2009) worked the soil and tended the animals of a South Dakota farm, planted and pastored a church in Southern California, and completed a PhD degree in theology with Thomas F. Torrance in New College Edinburgh. He began his professional teaching career at Westmont College, and then taught and served in various administrative capacities at Fuller Theological Seminary for thirty-three years (retiring as Professor Emeritus of Theology and Ministry). While teaching at Fuller, he served as a parish pastor, always insisting that theology and ministry go hand-in-hand.

The pastoral theologian who began his teaching career in middle age penned twenty-seven books. Like Karl Barth, Prof. Anderson articulated a theology of and for the church based on God's own ministry of revelation and reconciliation in the world. As professor and pastor, he modeled an incarnational, evangelical passion for the healing of humanity by Jesus Christ, who is *both* God's self-revelation to us *and* the reconciliation of our broken humanity to the triune God. His gift of relating suffering and alienated humans to Christ existing as community (Dietrich Bonhoeffer) is a recurrent motif throughout his life, ministry, and works.

The Ray S. Anderson Collection comprises books by Ray Anderson, an introductory text to his theology by Christian D. Kettler, two edited volumes that celebrate his distinguished academic career (*Incarnational Ministry: The Presence of Christ in Church, Society, and Family* and *On Being Christian . . . and Human*), and a reprint of an Edification volume that focuses on Ray Anderson's contributions to the field of Christian Psychology. A word of gratitude is due to The Society of Christian Psychology and its parent organization, The American Association for Christian Counselors, for their permission to make the *Edification* issue available in book form. Jim Tedrick of Wipf and Stock Publishers deserves a special word of thanks for publishing many of Ray Anderson's books and commissioning this collection of works to continue his legacy.

Todd H. Speidell, General Editor

EDIFICATION
JOURNAL OF THE SOCIETY FOR CHRISTIAN PSYCHOLOGY

Volume 1 • Issue 2 • 2007

EDIFICATION
Journal of the Society for Christian Psychology

Executive Editors
Timothy A. Sisemore, Ph.D.
Psychological Studies Institute
tsisemore@psy.edu

P.J. Watson, Ph.D.
University of Tennessee at Chattanooga
Paul-Watson@utc.edu

Consulting Editors
Alvin Dueck, Ph.D.
Fuller Theological Seminary

Robert C. Roberts, Ph.D.
Baylor University

C. Stephen Evans, Ph.D.
Baylor University

Mark R. Talbot, Ph.D.
Wheaton College

Eric L. Johnson, Ph.D.
Southern Baptist Theological Seminary

Siang-Yang Tan, Ph.D.
Fuller Theological Seminary

Michael W. Mangis, Ph.D.
Wheaton College

Alan Tjeltveit, Ph.D.
Muhlenberg College

Philip G. Monroe, Psy.D.
Biblical Seminary

Robert A. Watson, Ph.D.
Wheaton College

Matthew Phelps, Ph.D
Malone College

Richard Winter, M.D.
Covenant Theological Seminary

Editorial Assistant
Diane Monteleone
Psychological Studies Institute
edification@psy.edu

Wipf and Stock Publishers
199 W 8th Ave, Suite 3
Eugene, OR 97401

ISBN 13: 978-1-60899-396-3
Publication date 1/15/2010

Edification Journal, 2007, Volume 1, Issue 2
Edification Journal is published by the American Association of Christian Counselors.

SCP Director: Eric Johnson
Managing Editor: Mark Camper
Art Director: Melanie Rebsamen
Advertising Director: Michael Queen
AACC President: Tim Clinton

The American Association of Christian Counselors is chartered in Virginia and dedicated to promoting excellence and unity in Christian counseling. The purpose and objectives of AACC and the programs that it sponsors are strictly informative, educational, and affiliative.

Views expressed by the authors, presenters, and advertisers are their own and do not necessarily reflect those of the Society for Christian Psychology, or the American Association of Christian Counselors. The Edification Journal, Society for Christian Psychology, and the AACC do not assume responsibility in any way for members' or subscribers' efforts to apply or utilize information, suggestions, or recommendations made by the organization, the publications, or other resources. All rights reserved. Copyright 2007.

If you have comments or questions about the content of the Edification Journal, please direct them to the Edification Director, Dr. Eric Johnson, P.O. Box 739, Forest, VA 24551.

Member Services: 1.800.526.8673, fax: 1.434.525.9480, www.AACC.net.

Copyright © 2007 by Christian Counseling Resources, Inc.

CONTENTS
Volume 1 | Issue 2 | 2007

Special Issue: The Work of Ray S. Anderson
Todd H. Speidell, Guest Editor

Dialogue on Christian Psychology

Discussion Article
Toward a Holistic Psychology: Putting all the Pieces in their Proper Place 5
Ray S. Anderson

Commentaries
A Holistically Psychological Response to Anderson 17
Jeffrey P. Bjorck

Response to Anderson's "Toward a Holistic Psychology" 20
Don Browning

A Winning Hand? Reflections on Ray Anderson's "Toward a Holistic Psychology" 23
Trey Buchanan

Toward a Holistic Psychology: Enriching the Puzzle – a Perichoretic Response 24
Graham Buxton

A Few Thoughts on the Applied Side of Anderson's Holistic Psychology 26
Marv Erisman

Anderson's Encounter with Kierkegaard 28
C. Stephen Evans

Respecting Ourselves as Christian Therapists 29
Deborah van Deusen Hunsinger

The Emerging or Co-Constructed Self: A Key Piece of the Puzzle 32
Cynthia Neal Kimball

The 'Third' Element in Mutual Encounter as Existence before God is Jesus Christ 35
Andrew Purves

Holistic Spirituality? Response to Ray Anderson 36
LeRon Shults

Living in the Space Between Us 37
John Swinton

Author's Response
An Edifying Evening Seminar...40
Ray S. Anderson

Articles
Advocate and Judge: The Vicarious Humanity of Christ and the "Ideal" Self..................49
Christian D. Kettler

The Necessity of a Christocentric Anthropology for Christian Psychology:
Reflections on Ray Anderson's Doctrine of Humanity 57
Mark A. Wells

Interview with Ray S. Anderson: Toward a Christian Theoanthropology.........................65
Ray S. Anderson and Todd H. Speidell

Book Reviews
Edifying Christian Psychology: Book Reviews 73
Timothy A. Sisemore, Editor

Dialogue on Christian Psychology: Discussion Article

Toward a Holistic Psychology: Putting all the Pieces in their Proper Place

Ray S. Anderson
Fuller Theological Seminary

Christians who are psychologists have often been reluctant to speak of having a Christian psychology—a hesitancy which assumes that the discipline of psychology should be "value-free" or at least free of religious concepts and practice. This article presents an alternative to that dichotomy by arguing that a holistic psychology is derived from a scientific understanding of "whole persons" as having an intrinsic spiritual core that is nonreligious, though with the potential for religious expression. The article concludes with some examples of how Christians who are psychologists can function in this nonreligious way with authentic spiritual integrity and with biblical authority.

During my first year of teaching at a Christian college in 1973, a professor of psychology invited me to give a lecture in his class on personality theory. I gave a lecture on personhood, remembering Karl Barth's (1960, p. 110) warning that personality is but a phenomenon, and as such, does not yet contain the essence of the "subject" that constitutes the "object" of psychology. Following the class, my colleague expressed some consternation and told me that we could not be farther apart in our methodology and that my attempt to bring psychology under the discipline of a Christian anthropology would only serve to undermine psychology as a scientific endeavor. He attempted to make his point by saying that, while an auto mechanic may be a Christian, there was no such thing as "Christian auto mechanics." While I agreed, I responded by saying that if you want to use that analogy, you appear to be more interested in the vehicle's mechanics while I am more concerned about the driver.

We agreed to disagree. But it was then that I realized the difference between a Christian who also happens to be a psychologist and a psychologist committed to the "science" of understanding the nature of the object (subject) under investigation. A true scientific method, my former mentor, Thomas Torrance (1965, p. 61), liked to say, develops when the nature of the object to be known determines the method of knowing.

Moving to Fuller Theological Seminary in 1976, I began to team-teach integration seminars with faculty from the Graduate School of Psychology and did so each year for twenty-five years. What emerged through those years was a deeper understanding of the relation of psychology as a discipline of study to psychotherapy and counseling as the praxis of healing persons. I discovered that the premise lying behind the attempts to integrate theology and psychology was that they were first of all disintegrated, each having its own pieces of a puzzle that were not cut from the same picture. The best that could be achieved was the creation of an interdisciplinary dialogue in which each discipline was to be respected. The search for the "missing piece" that would put it all together could not be found—for in theory it did not exist. The whole was always more than the sum total of the parts.

While my training was in theology and the curriculum of my faculty was oriented toward pastoral ministry, I began to see that from both sides of the street (literally!) the same students were nonetheless crossing over even though our curricula had no connecting bridge. Not only were the students the same person, whether theology or psychology students, but the persons that each would eventually encounter in actual practice were also the same person. I wanted to find out, "Who is this person?" If Torrance was right, the science of psychology and the science of theology had in view the same subject to which each was bound to understand as the objective basis for whatever was determined to be "true" as well as "good." This relation is what I later explored under the theme of the isomorphic relation between the science of psychology and the science of theology (Anderson, 1989). "Isomorphic" can be understood as "similarity in organisms of different ancestry resulting from convergence." Theology and psychology reveal their isomorphic qualities when they converge on the nature and meaning of human selfhood as being-in-the-world. But I run ahead.

It was at Fuller Seminary that I heard Viktor Frankl (1959, 1977), the founder of Logotherapy, speak and urge upon us a vision of the human person where spirit (will to meaning) was as much a factor in the human experience as were the physical (somatic) and emotional (psychological). He discovered the reality of the spiritual dimension of human psychology, not in a classroom but in a death camp.

He seemed to have all the pieces; only assembly was required.

It was at Fuller that I heard O. Hobart Mowrer (1961, p. 50) lecture and expand on his thesis that "sin is the lesser of two evils." Some persons carry guilt feelings, Mowrer told us, because they may very well be actually guilty. Some form of atonement may be as necessary as reducing guilt feelings through therapeutic intervention. To hear the former president of the American Psychological Association suggest that becoming a whole person through a religious experience of confession and forgiveness was welcome news to the theologians present, but his message perplexed some of the psychologists.

It was at Fuller that I heard Paul Tournier (1957) lecture and reveal the fact that in his own counseling he discovered the "meaning of being a person" when, in a moment of frustration, he shared with his client some of his own pain. At that moment, Tournier said, when he became a real person rather than merely an objective, remote therapist, this woman responded by saying, "So then you and I have something in common!" Her movement to recovery and wellbeing began at that very moment, Tournier told us. And he reiterated the point by telling us that behind every psychological problem exists a real person, and only another person can touch the soul of a person who is suffering. So the psychologist is a person too!

And then there was Kierkegaard. It was Edward Carnell, my former teacher at Fuller who introduced me to Kierkegaard in a course that later was to become his book, *The Burden of Søren Kierkegaard* (Carnell, 1965). In the years following, I read virtually everything the melancholy Dane had written. I learned from him what it meant to be the self in the constant dialectic of freedom and necessity, the eternal and the temporal. He taught me that one reaches faith only by passing through dread; that despair is the enemy of faith because it is the absence of dread; and that the self cannot be the self without placing itself in relation to God, an action which causes one to experience dread. Dread increases guilt, Kierkegaard said, by making guilt infinite, not susceptible to temporal (finite) mediation, but only to find freedom (repose) in atonement. Having said this, he ended his discourse by saying, "So soon as psychology has finished with dread, it has nothing to do but to deliver it over to dogmatics" (Kierkegaard, 1944, p. 145).

What did he mean by this statement? I had thought that by walking hand in hand with Kierkegaard I had come to the place that theology left me longing for. Was it not enough to find the self within the person? True, Kierkegaard reminded us that the self cannot posit itself as the self without being open to the other, but it turns out that this "other" lies on the other side of dread; only the divine "other" can keep faith from falling back into despair. The most significant human relation that he experienced was his engagement to Regina Olsen, an "instant love affair" that lasted for several years until he ended it by his own decision, for her own good, as he put it, even though he continued to love her. In the end, while he could apparently surrender everything to the infinite for the sake of faith, he did not have the kind of faith that permitted him to enact a finite relation of love without losing his own self. "Had I had faith I would have remained with Regina" (Kierkegaard, 1958, p. 86)!

Having become a self through the solitary "narrow pass" of the individual, Kierkegaard embraced the way like clinging to a life raft with only enough room for one in the midst of a sea of struggling souls. He wrote of his own task in life as that of an "unimportant servant who, if possible, was to help the masses trying to go through the narrow pass, 'the individual.' Yet had I to crave an inscription on my grave I would ask for none other than 'the individual'—and even if it is not understood now, then in truth it will be" (Kierkegaard, 1958, p. 133).

In leaving behind Kierkegaard in my search for the "whole" of the human person, I was reminded of Carnell's (1957) own lament when he found that his bent toward a more rational apologetic led him to abandon his journey with Kierkegaard. "Now that I had to part company with the Dane, I felt somewhat like a wayfarer who, having come a long distance by himself, is suddenly joined by one going to the same country; only to find that when they unexpectedly confront a fork in the road, each adamantly defies the judgment of the other. In the end they must go their separate ways, for each tenaciously clings to his own convictions" (Carnell, 79). For myself, it was not so much a fork in the road as a "divided highway" with Kierkegaard always within view, if not also within conversational distance! Carnell may have had his own demons that caused him to turn away from Kierkegaard. I was just looking for better angels to guide me while Kierkegaard preferred to walk on a path where only one could pass at a time. And I still remembered Kierkegaard's warning that he could only expose the inner workings of a finite soul tormented by the infinite (the limitations of psychology); it would be up to others to trace out the contours of a personal human self "before the fall," as it were, persons who experience "being the self" as derived out of "being for others."

I thought that Stephen Evans would point the way. Evans clearly is indebted to Kierkegaard as evidenced by his early writings where his concern for the self as a free and ethical agent led him subsequently to Kierkegaard (Evans, 1977, 1990, 1998, 2006). While his early work was mainly directed at recovering the individual agent from positivistic human sciences, he was not reticent even then to mention the social aspect of persons. "The Bible never views a person purely as a passive product of these social roles. He is, still, in the midst of these roles, a responsible agent. He becomes what he becomes in the context of these social roles which tremendously limit and weight his options as an agent. Nevertheless, as a rational, responsible agent, he is not merely formed by these social relationships; he acts and by acting helps to form these roles in turn. He is not only constituted by these relationships; he himself constitutes them. He plays a role in continuing them, modifying them for better or worse, enhancing or degrading their quality and character" (Evans 1977, p. 145).

Clearly Evans wants to establish a view of the human self that is as much social as individual, but in doing so, following Kierkegaard, he attempts to begin with the individual as the core self in relation to another. Kierkegaard, says Evans (1990), defined the self as "a relation that relates itself to itself." But the self cannot constitute its own self; Evans goes on to cite Kierkegaard, "the human self is a derived, established relation, a relation that relates itself to itself, and in relating itself to itself relates itself to another" (Evans, 1990, pp. 13-14). But what does it mean to say that the self is "established by another" or that the self "relates itself to another"? In my opinion, Kierkegaard is referring to God in the above passages cited by Evans. God establishes the self in a dialectical relation that, in the process of relating itself to itself, relates itself back to God. Kierkegaard himself admits, as Evans acknowledges, that it is God who established man in relation (Evans, 1990, p. 16). In addition, in the discourse that follows these introductory pages, very little is said of the self relating socially to another person as an essential part of the definition of the self. It thus appears that Kierkegaard intends to ground the ontological self as a dialectic relation established by God. Nonetheless, Evans wants to push Kierkegaard beyond the dialectical self as existing essentially before God prior to actual social relationships. Evans' (1988b) writings on "Kierkegaard's View of the Unconscious" as well as *Søren Kierkegaard's Christian Psychology* (Evans, 1990), all argue for a relational view of the self, which he perceives as found in Kierkegaard.

Peter Young (1991, p. 39) argues that, while Kierkegaard relegates the social to an ethical possibility and not an ontological part of the core self, Evans appears to drop the dialectical relation for the sake of a more ontological sense of a relational self. In the final analysis, though, one wonders whether Evans truly engages with Kierkegaard's existential self-as-agent. In *Preserving the Person* (Evans, 1977), Evans presents the self as individually forming and shaping the community of which it is a part. In *Søren Kierkegaard's Christian Psychology*, Evans (1990) appears to view social being as not only the goal of true selfhood, but also a core aspect of the "pre-self" in Kierkegaard's model. This view may read back into Kierkegaard more than he can allow without compromising the "singularity" of the mediation of the eternal into the temporal.

In his lonely trek along the narrow pass, I fear that Kierkegaard will look back over his shoulder to see Evans following behind him rather than by his side, shoulder to shoulder. The narrow pass admits only one at a time. Meanwhile, I have found other friends.

Beyond Denmark to Scotland and Germany

During my doctoral study in Edinburgh in 1970-72, I had several meetings with John Macmurray to discuss his concept of personhood, having read his early work on *Reason and Emotion* (Macmurray, 1935) and his two-volume work published from the Gifford Lectures in Scotland, *The Self as Agent* (Macmurray, 1957) and *Persons in Relation* (Macmurray, 1961). What was of particular interest to me was Macmurray's concept of the person as constituted through encounter with the (human) Other. He argued that the *self* is not formed by thinking but by acting. By substituting the self in place of the person, he made a formal shift in the emphasis between the theoretical and the practical (Macmurray, 1961, pp. 26-27). By insisting on the primacy of the practical and adopting the perspective of the *agent* rather than the *subject*, Macmurray overcame the antimony between freedom and determinism (Kierkegaard's dialectic). In other words, the self as agent cannot exist in a personal sense in isolation; action as a form of the personal cannot exist apart from the Other, who as a fellow agent offers the *resistance* necessary for the act to be personal (Macmurray, 1961, pp. 108-109). The reality of a person is in his or her action with the Other because action entails individuality as a consequence of the act. When individuality assumes the primary role, Macmurray argued, the self will either assume a passive or an aggressive role in the relation, but in either case, "personal" relation is not possible (Macmurray 1961, p. 137). Only when I transcend my individuality in actual encounter with the Other do I meet the necessary "resistance" by which my individuality becomes personal. Only resistance by another personal agent (as a social encounter) can save my individuality from the isolation of the impersonal. The freedom of self-transcendence and the freedom to relate to the other are not opposed as a dialectic but united in action. "To act, then, as the essential unity of these two freedoms is to modify the Other by intention. To this we add that since the agent is part of the Other, he cannot modify the Other without modifying himself, or know the Other without knowing himself. In determining the future for the Other he also determines his own future" (Macmurray 1961, p. 166). This is where Macmurray, more than Kierkegaard, appears to support Evan's concept of the self.

An interactive relation with another person, says Macmurray, is essential for development of the self. "I need you to be myself. This need is for a fully positive personal relation in which, because we trust one another, we can think and feel and act together. Only in such a relation can we really be ourselves. If we quarrel, each of us withdraws from the Other into himself, and the trust is replaced by fear. We can no longer be ourselves in relation to one another" (Macmurray 1961, p. 150). Macmurray goes on to say that when we are in conflict with one another only reconciliation which restores the original confidence and trust can overcome the negative motivation which results in hostility. Apart from this kind of reconciliation we remain isolated individuals. "What we really need," he suggests, "is to care for one another, and we are only caring for ourselves. We have achieved society, but not community. We have become associates, but not friends" (Macmurray 1961, p. 150). The achievement of community of persons is grounded in actions that embody intentionality to share a common "soul" or a common history and a common destiny. Macmurray adds: "The inherent ideal of the personal is a community of persons in which each cares for all the others, and no one cares for himself" (Macmurray 1961, p. 159).

Balswick, King, and Reimer (2005) have developed Macmurray's reciprocal aspect of personhood in their recent book, *The Reciprocating Self*. They suggest that the image of God constitutes a reciprocal relationship at the human level analogous to humans' relation to God. "Following the pattern of the trinitarian relationships, such relationships are characterized by mutuality, give and take, and they enable the self to be known most fully in the process of knowing another" (Balswick et al. 2005, p. 36).

Macmurray's construction of the form of the personal along the lines of the I-Thou relation obviously paralleled the thought of Martin Buber (1970) and raises the question of Macmurray's dependence upon Buber. I put the question to him in a personal interview in 1971. He responded by saying that he had worked out his own concepts of the person before reading Buber, but he felt that both concepts were proceeding along similar lines. The difference, he said, was that he (Macmurray) placed the emphasis on the act of reciprocity that constitutes both the self and the other in reality, while Buber stressed the "space" between the I-Thou encounter as that which constitutes the person. In this regard, Macmurray told me with a twinkle in his eye, "Buber was more of a poet than a philosopher. His concept of the person was a wee bit too mystical for my liking."

With Macmurray I found the form of the personal as the essential core of the self, which as I construed it, was both existential because it was the self existing in relation to the other and social because it was the self constituted by the other. I viewed Macmurray as saying to Kierkegaard, "Go ahead and marry Regina; you will find more of your self in living with her than in loving her." The psychological self, by itself, can never rise to the level of intentionality. This was the push I needed to get beyond Kierkegaard, but there was still something missing.

My attention switched from Scotland to Germany. Dietrich Bonhoeffer was a younger contemporary of Macmurray. The two never met and did not interact or correspond, to my knowledge. Yet they have in common a view of the self that is based on a social construct of personal and mutual interaction. In a work that is extraordinary in light of his youth and precocious insight, Dietrich Bonhoeffer (1998) at the age of 21 wrote his doctoral dissertation at the University of Berlin. In my estimation, this dissertation accomplished what no other work since has achieved in the integration of spirituality, sociality, and human personhood. While his dissertation was ostensibly an attempt to define the nature of the church, he began with a creative and profound examination of the social nature of human personhood as the basis for stating his thesis that Jesus Christ exists in the spiritual structure of human sociality as community (*Gemeinde*) rather than in the institutional form of the church. This work was published in 1927, before Buber (1970) had written his classic work, *I and Thou*, and a decade before Macmurray's (1935) seminal work, *Reason and Emotion*.

Bonhoeffer's father, Karl, was head of the psychiatry faculty at the University of Berlin and strenuously rejected the contemporary psychoanalytic field of psychiatry represented by Freud and Jung. His emphasis was more empirical than analytical. "The theoretical interpretation of what was *behind* that being observed, of what occurred unconsciously and might project itself into consciousness, was foreign to his approach" (Bethge, 2000, p. 22). Dietrich was certainly well aware of the various theoretical approaches in the discipline of psychology, but due to his father's influence, no doubt, later in life reacted almost with disgust at what he called the "pernicious" probing at a person's inner life by the existentialist philosophers and psychotherapists who "set themselves to drive people to inward despair, and then the game is in their hands. That is secularized methodism" (Bonhoeffer 1971, p. 326). In a letter written from prison in 1944, Bonhoeffer reflected on influences that led to transitions in his life and said that one important factor was "the first conscious influence of father's personality. It was then I turned from phraseology to reality" (Bethge 2000, p. 203).

It is quite clear that Bonhoeffer's interest was more in the "person" than in the self, which led him to draw from some of the contemporary social theorists rather than psychologists in his early work. Although Ferdinand Ebner is often cited as source for his personalist psychology, there is no evidence that he was acquainted with Ebner's work at this stage. He apparently drew upon the philosopher Eberhard Griesback though also criticized him for attempting to make the I-You relationship absolute and so lapsing back into idealism. He sought to overcome this lapse by grounding the interpersonal construct of humanity in sociality (Bethge 2000, p. 83). Thus, sociology rather than philosophy became his primary source for developing his concept of the person. At the outset of his dissertation, he established his thesis in the following formula: "Our concern here is the relationship of the person, God, and social being to each other" (Bonhoeffer 1998, p. 54). He elaborated on this concept with respect to the relation of the individual to the community. "God does not desire a history of individual human beings, but the history of the *human* community. However, God does not want a community that absorbs the individual into itself, but a community of *human beings*. In God's eyes, community and individual exist in the same moment and rest in one another. The collective unit and the individual unit have the same structure in God's eyes" (Bonhoeffer 1998, p. 80). While this idea became the underlying basis for his theology of the church as a concrete social unit before it could be considered a religious institution, what emerged was, in effect, a "holistic psychology" that included physicality (embodiment), mutuality (affect, will), and spirituality (individuality). "The social basic category is the I-You relation. The You of the other person is the divine You. Thus the way to the other person's You is the same as the way to the divine You, either through acknowledgment or rejection. The individual becomes a person over and again through the other, in the 'moment.' The other person presents us with the same challenge to our knowing as does God" (Bonhoeffer 1998, pp. 55-56).

Where Macmurray stopped with the concept of "resistance" constituted by encounter with the other, Bonhoeffer carried this concept one step farther by positing a "third" element in the mutual encounter that he called "objective spirit" or "objective person." "Two wills encountering one another form a structure. A third person joining them sees not just one person connected to the other; rather, the will of the structure, as a third factor, resists the newcomer with a resistance not identical with the wills of the two individuals. Sometimes this is even more powerful than that of either individual—or than the sum of all the individuals, if this is at all conceivable. Precisely this structure is objective spirit" (Bonhoeffer 1998, p. 98).

When the self comes into relation with another, a mutual will is formed that results in a psychic and spiritual unity. The presence of one self to another can be experienced as "resistance," with the other forming an opportunity for relation or for opposition. The active will of the other in the relation is a form of resistance that we experience in others, either in a positive or negative form. This resistance provides an objective basis for our own subjectivity, so that our sense of self is based on a practical and not merely theoretical concept. Another way of saying it is that we cannot experience true subjectivity apart from the encounter and relation with other subjects.

This construct of the person became the basis for understanding how the Holy Spirit (or Christ) can abide in human persons without creating a religious dimension alongside the human. His "holistic psychology," as I have called it, was in effect, a "nonreligious" spirituality within a psychological construct of the person. "The objective spirit, fraught with so much contingency, imperfection, and sin, nevertheless has the promise that it can preach the word of God; it becomes the bearer of the social activity of the Holy Spirit" (Bonhoeffer 1998, p. 233).

Because the reality of spirit is first of all a social reality rooted in the nature of human personhood, Bonhoeffer holds that the social structure of human personhood is intrinsically spiritual. The Spirit of God does not constitute something alongside of or merely inside of a person as an individual. Rather, the Spirit of God joins the human spirit at the core of its social reality. "The individual personal spirit lives solely by virtue of sociality. Only in interaction with one another is the spirit of human beings ever revealed; this is the essence of spirit, to be oneself through being in the other" (1998, 73). Structural openness to other persons, said Bonhoeffer, is not only necessary for the development of one's self-identity, but is also the basis for our own spiritual identity. Spirituality is thus contingent upon social being as prior to and the foundation for religious instincts and experiences. In this sense, one could say along with Teilhard de Chardin: "We are not human beings having a spiritual experience, but spiritual beings having a human experience" (McDonald, 1994, p. 76).

Bonhoeffer viewed the self as personal being, structurally open to others as well as structurally closed (Bonhoeffer, 1998, pp. 65, 75). By this he meant that individuality is derived out of community. Being open to the spirit of other persons awakens and intensifies one's own spirit. Personal being is structurally open and closed. There is no self-consciousness without consciousness of the other, that is, of community. "In God's eyes, community and individual exist in the same moment and rest in one another" (Bonhoeffer 1998, p. 80). Grounding spirituality in the basic social structure of human being, he added, "Individual personal spirit lives solely by virtue of sociality, and 'social spirit' becomes real only in individual formation; thus genuine sociality itself presses toward personal unity. One cannot speak of the priority of either personal or social being" (Bonhoeffer 1998, p. 75). The relational spirituality suggested by Bonhoeffer has been developed further by Shults and Sandage (2006), who say that interpersonal tensions in relation with others can often be negative as well as positive, resulting in spiritual impairment. These interpersonal conflicts can become "opportunities for relational growth and healing, but this requires work and wise guidance." By analogy, these kinds of relational struggles can also occur with respect to the self's relation with God (Shults & Sandage, pp. 221-225).

Assembling the Pieces of the Puzzle
I think that we now have all the pieces. What is required is some assembly! Kierkegaard forced the self out of hiding (despair) so that through dread, "spirit" can emerge as the connective link with God. While dread (*angst*) is the precondition for sin (Kierkegaard 1944, p. 82), it is also the precondition for faith. Dread "educates" faith by confronting the self with the infinite Spirit of God as the only possibility, and thus "spirit" emerges. Without dread as a psychological state of the self, one cannot experience spirit as a spiritual form of the self (Kierkegaard 1944, p. 141). Without dread there can be no spirit; the deeper the dread, the more powerful the spirit. This is what Ernest Becker (1973) seized upon when he found that the root of all neurosis and pathology of the self could be found in Kierkegaard's concept of dread, which Becker interpreted as existential fear of our own mortality, rather than Freud's ego-psychology based on infantile sexuality trauma. This piece of the puzzle can be called the psychology of faith.

Stephen Evans provided another piece with his development of the concept of agency as a core element of the self, by which the self makes choices, holds values, and achieves personhood as orientation toward the other. In this way, persons are both free and responsible for their actions. Evans reminds us that there can be no "value-free" psychology precisely because of the self's impulse toward meaning, that is, toward an achievement of the self beyond mere self-existence. The psychology of personal freedom, along with an intuitive sense of moral wisdom, contributes another piece.

From Macmurray (1935), we discover the objective nature of personhood based on mutual subjectivity in relation. Thus, love integrates the self objectively, not subjectively. Emotions in the form of feelings are rational in that they are directed toward the objective reality of the other subject. The psychology of individuality is derivative of mutual intentionality in community.

With Dietrich Bonhoeffer, the puzzle begins to come together. While searching for a social hermeneutic by which to account for the religious community (the church), he discovered instead a spiritual hermeneutic which bound together personal existence, social existence, and existence before God in the world without dependence upon religion. His letters from prison, written under what came to be an inevitable "deadline" of personal existence, reveal an extraordinary state of psychological health that can only be attributed to what might be called the "self-therapy" of nonreligious faith. He came to the conclusion that the church has failed, religion has failed, and so in all honesty we must realize that our lives can no longer be held together by concepts of a metaphysical God. "And we cannot be honest unless we recognize that we have to live in the world *etsi deus non duretur* [even if there were no God]. And this is just what we do recognize—before God! God himself compels us to recognize it . . . God would have us know that we must live as men who manage our lives without him. The God who lets us live in the world without the working hypothesis of God is the God before whom we stand continually. Before God and with God we live without God" (Bonhoeffer 1971, p. 360).

His former student and biographer, Eberhard Bethge (2000), tells us that during Bonhoeffer's most active and successful life before being imprisoned, he suffered recurring episodes of psychological distress or "spiritual trial" (*accidia* and *tristia*). Most often these attacks came following times when he had been most successful in lecturing or leading others, but once in prison, Bethge says, these episodes never occurred again (Bethge, p. 833). He gained his psychological health in living out his theological hope. His psychology of socially embedded spirituality may well be the missing piece. It is time to assemble the parts.

A Coherent Construal of Personhood

I am guided methodologically by Barth's insistence that behind the phenomenon of the self (personality) there is a subject that is the object to be known. Torrance suggested that the method by which we know something is determined by the nature of the object to be known. We have discovered several parts that belong to this subject, the self existing in a dialectic of despair and faith, the self as agent, the self in relation, and the self as core spiritual being. In looking for a conceptual model I have borrowed a phrase from Walter Brueggemann (1993): "A young person must have a coherent construal of reality, so that all the parts make sense in a whole" (p. 98). It is not enough to *think* about the person who is the subject of both psychology and theology; we must be able to give a *coherent construal* of that subject. For example, Anthony Greenwald created the term *"personalysis"* (parallel to *psychoanalysis*) to indicate indebtedness to Freud's approach. The elements that constitute the set of subsystems of the self describe a pre-theoretical or meta-theoretical model, rather than having well-defined referents. While Freud's theory of the id, ego, and superego provided an analysis of the *psyche* (mind), Greenwald proposed an analysis of the *person* into subsystems (1982, p. 152). I am proposing a pre-theoretical model of personhood as a way of construing the various elements or spheres of personal being that constitute the person.

My attempt in developing the pre-theoretical model is to get behind theories about human spirituality and mental health to the core of personhood itself. Of necessity, my model resembles the wiring diagram of a computer's circuits and appears abstract when viewed apart from the day-to-day life of persons. At the same time, however, as with paradigms used by physicists, my model directs us toward the objective reality of persons rather than away from them. Therapeutic strategies as well as strategies and techniques of spiritual formation will invariably fail unless integrated by the self's own inner cohesion and unity.

In developing this model, I begin with what the Bible tells us (Genesis 1): humans were created out of the dust of the ground (physical), into which the Creator breathed the breath of life (mental), and finally endowed them with the divine image (spiritual). From this biblical account, and from empirical experience, I construe humans to be created as having both mental and physical existence within which the actual self is *composed* in relation to God and others. When I project this into a coherent construal of the human person, it results in a developmental and integrative model.

We enter into life as infants held in a social relation to parenting persons. We are not yet differentiated as "persons" with a self-identity that exists over and against others or even "it." Further development entails sexual differentiation with gender identity assimilated into the core self-identity, again with respect to the sexual and personal identity of other persons. The development of psychical experience and capacity comes later, with a deeper capacity to feel and express feelings and emotions. The growth of the self does not "add" stages as it develops, but the dimension of the self in each sphere is enlarged and becomes more functional. The psychical life of the infant, for example, is present from birth, and no doubt before. At the same time, the entire spectrum of the psychical range of feelings and experiences is quite limited. Children cry when they experience pain, both physically and mentally, but they do not weep out of the depth of sadness of which an adult is capable. Children experience joy and feelings of happiness, but they have not yet developed a depth of joy that is able to integrate pain and loss into that joy. We could think of human persons as constituted by a set of subsystems, systemically related. That is, each subsystem, with its relative autonomy that makes up the human person, is part of a whole—which is more than the sum of the parts.

A pre-theoretical schematic diagram can be constructed which shows the way in which components of the self as individual and relational can be viewed. A schematic diagram is somewhat like a wiring diagram for a television or computer. It is not intended to show which buttons to push in order to operate the thing. Rather, it reveals how each system is connected, so that if a malfunction occurs a trained technician knows where to locate the problem. Figure 1 below is just such a 'wiring diagram' for the human person and is meant to be read accordingly.

Figure 1 Systems of the Self

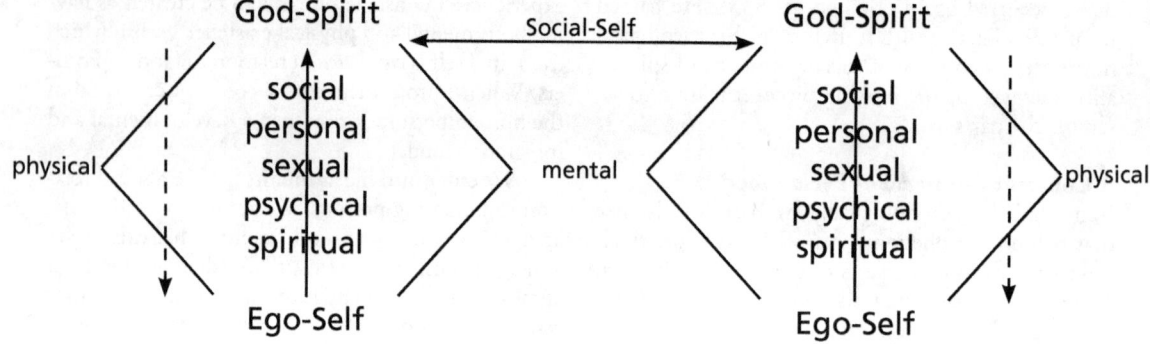

Reading from top to bottom (dotted line), we see that the progression is from social to personal to sexual to psychical and finally to spiritual. As spiritual beings, we then have an orientation to God as Spirit which runs right back through each of the other subsets or subsystems of the self. The dotted line represents the growth of the self through each of the spheres, beginning with the social and moving toward the spiritual. The solid line moves from the self through each sphere toward God. This depicts the integration of the self as the self and in relation to the other. The physical and mental aspects of personal life impinge upon each of the spheres, and the physical and mental health of each has an effect upon the spheres.

These systemic components are not "stages" through which one passes developmentally in a strict linear fashion. Rather, the model should be viewed more like a spiral staircase, where one continues to make progress developmentally but with each "rotation" through the process enters into and experiences each "system" from a more mature (one hopes!) perspective.

It will also be noted that there is both an individual "ego-self" and a relational "ego-self" in this model. This is meant to convey the fact that both individuality and relationality are essential to a holistic psychology of the self. One could also construe this as the ego-self having both a vertical and horizontal contingent relation to the other—Divine and human. In theological terms, this is expressed by the concept of the image of God as described in the creation account. When it is said, "It is not good that the man should be alone" (Genesis 2:18), it is the horizontal relational aspect that is lacking. Relation with God as the Creator on the part of the solitary individual is thus to be construed as insufficient to complete the divine image in a human person. The diagram above is meant to portray this in schematic form.

The above figure also attempts to preserve a balance and positive tension between the physical and mental aspects of the personality for each of the components. Rather than viewing the physical and mental aspects of the self as a polarity, each contributes to and participates in the several spheres of the self. In other words, the spiritual sphere of the self, for instance, should be not be viewed either as purely mental or physical, for the spirituality of the self draws upon both the physical and mental in its integrative relation to the other spheres. For example, if one should view the spiritual dimension primarily as a mental aspect of the self, spirituality will tend to become either rationalistic or mystical, both of which are essentially movements away from the concreteness and embodiment of the self. Spirituality is part of the holistic psychology of the self as portrayed in the figure above. Each of the spheres, the spiritual, psychical, sexual, personal and social, *form* the self in such a way that the physical and mental aspects are drawn together so as to contribute to the self's internal and external unity and integration in a holistic and healthy way.

In a sense, one could say that when the self tends toward either the physical or mental aspect, the two kinds of despair described by Kierkegaard (1980) come into play. That is, when the self turns toward either the physical or the mental as a primary mode of being, the self is "unwilling to be the self." However, as Kierkegaard also pointed out, in "willing to be the self," a sense of dread (*angst*) is experienced that can only be overcome by a movement of the self toward God as Spirit. Thus, he argued, spirit emerges out of dread as an existential act.

In my model, spirit is present at the core of the self, and thus the self finds its meaning and value (Evans, 1989) in moving through the entire self toward God as agent. The diagram shows that the self is not merely an individual but is "composed" through relationality with other persons (Macmurray, 1961, Balswick, 2005). What makes this construal of human personhood coherent is the spiritual bond among the self, persons, and God (Bonhoeffer, 1998). In this way "spirit" is transforming in its relationality (Shults and Sandage, 2006).

The developmental model depicted in Figure 1 thus has a two-fold dimension. There is a vertical integration of the self as personal being through each of the spheres, with an ego-self-identity that includes appropriate mental and physical self-reference. This developmental process requires constant adjustment to the ego-self as changes occur both inwardly and with reference to the embodied life of the self. At the same time, there is a developmental process where integration of the ego-self with the relational-self must take place through the changes that are occurring in the social dimension of personal experience. This integrative project and process contributes to the unity of the self provided that it takes place in a relatively healthy and holistic way. However, it should be remembered that the depiction of the ego-self and the relational-self is schematic and not intended to suggest that the self actually has two centers. Self-identity, as Meissner (1987) has pointed out, includes both the spiritual (individual) and social (relational) aspects of the one ego-self.

Toward a Holistic Psychology of Human Personhood

If this model achieves to some degree a holistic psychology by assembling all of the parts, it may offer a new perspective on psychological aspects of human personhood and, in particular, what I would call a "nonreligious Christian psychology." Of all the disciplines in the social and behavior sciences, psychology lies closest to the "heart" of humanity itself. If the spiritual core of a human self is present as a nonreligious phenomenon, as Kierkegaard, Evans, and especially Bonhoeffer have argued, psychology would be less than human and not entirely personal, if it chose to dismiss or ignore the spiritual dimension of personhood.

In the past, Christian psychology has attempted to recover this dimension by seeking to integrate the psychological with the religious self or, in a more academic environment, psychology and theology. I have attempted to show that such integrative attempts fail at the outset by identifying the spiritual dimension as a phenomenon of religiosity, having its own "measurement" scale and therapeutic outcomes. It was this attempt to "Christianize" psychology that led my colleague to construe my own version of personhood as eroding psychological objectivity. While there may well be value in research and analysis of religion as a subsection of psychology in general, confusion of religious expression with the core spiritual dimension of human personhood is a methodological failure, if not also a psychological mutant. Shults and Sandage (2006, pp. 155-156) help to clarify the confusion between spirituality and religion by defining religion, on the one hand, as a multidimensional construct including moral and spiritual practices. Spirituality, on the other hand, is increasingly becoming thought of as an experience of transcendence, or the sacred, separate from any established religion.

My hope is to reopen the dialogue with a more encompassing vision of what might be called Christian psychology as at least more competent in theory as well as practice than any other form of psychology, precisely because it is willing to consider the spiritual aspect of human personhood to belong to the "subject that is the object" of psychological interest. Thus I would define a 'well integrated' psychologist as having a multilevel competence in relating to the whole person. The fact that the spiritual dimension of the human person can and does lead to various religious expressions should not disqualify it any more than an intrinsic moral intuition of the self can often produce a variety of ethical systems. Yet, as Evans has shown, wisdom could be considered a pre-moral virtue. In the same way, I argue that spirituality is a pre-religious virtue. In fact, it is more than just a piece that fits into the puzzle; it is the profile (image) of which each piece is cut.

As a science, psychology develops its knowledge base out of actual observation and participation in the life experience of others, not least of all its therapeutic experience. As in theology, where the knowledge of God in the experience of salvation leads to knowledge of God in his own being, so in psychology, knowledge of the self as being emerges out of knowledge of the self as becoming. When psychology traces "affect" to the reality of being that produces the affect, it is already in the realm of spirit, not merely "mind." In so doing, it has already been "affected" by the teleological goals and values that contribute to change and growth toward wholeness on the part of the human self. This "knowledge through participation," as Polanyi (1974) liked to call it, opens up and transforms the science of knowing. The isomorphic factor (Anderson, 1989) that emerges as the convergence of theology and psychology has specifically to do with the teleological goal toward which the human self reaches and strives as essential to its being and true knowledge of self, the world, and God.

Moving from psychology to psychotherapy and counseling on this model requires what Deborah van Deusen Hunsinger (1995) calls a "bilingual" approach to the expressed concerns of a client. She argues that psychology and theology are quite distinct disciplines which have an asymmetrical relationship that gives theology a view of God's precedence (Barth) in defining the true nature of the human, but also allows for the integrity of the discipline of psychology (as with other disciplines) to explore aspects of the human which theology does not explicate. A therapist who can respond to persons as having disturbance in either spiritual or psychological sources is "bi-lingual," by her definition. In other words, while the essential core of the self is spiritual, not every pain experienced is spiritual pain. There are emotions, anxieties, and even mental disorders that "speak their own language." Other expressions of the self may be more specifically matters of the spirit, guilt, a sense of estrangement from God, and even feelings of being attacked or indwelt with evil or demonic powers. These aspects of the self speak their own language, Hunsinger maintains, and thus an effective therapist should be able to respond accordingly.

In my way of construing the self, the spiritual aspect as a nonreligious component is fully psychological as the human core of the self. A holistic psychology such as I have presented can include spirituality without having to use theological terminology or religious strategies of intervention and treatment, unless they are necessary or appropriate. Thus, holistic psychology can operate at the spiritual level in a nonreligious way as I have suggested in my book, *Spiritual Caregiving as Secular Sacrament* (Anderson, 2003). At the same time, from the perspective of a holistic Christian psychology, one can respond to expressed spiritual needs of the client with theological and religious strategies of healing. In my version, the bilingual aspect is not so much between theology and psychology as between a nonreligious and a religious spirituality, both of which are compatible with a holistic psychology and should be part of the competence of a psychologist who is a Christian.

Let's Talk

Can a Christian who is a psychologist deal with spirituality with a client who has or does not express a Christian belief system? I would say yes. For example, when Jesus encountered a Samaritan woman who was drawing water from a well and asked her for a drink, she raised the religious question of how he, a Jew and a male, could talk with a Samaritan and a woman. Sensing the spiritual, rather than the religious nature of her question, he responded with an analogy of "living water" that he could provide. After a brief conversation, she requested some of this water. He then asked her to call her husband, drawing her out of the "one-on-one" relationship with him into her closest social relationship. When she responded by saying she had no husband, Jesus, with spiritual (therapeutic) insight, revealed that he knew more than she intended to tell; she had had a series of relationships and was living with a man who was not her husband. His inquiry, instead of shaming her, brought forth another response of a religious nature regarding the authorized place of worship, to which Jesus responded in a nonreligious way, "God is spirit, and those who worship him must worship in spirit and in truth." The transforming nature of this spiritual encounter at a purely human level led her to confess that he was the Messiah (John 4:7:26).

This encounter is an example of the kind of bilingual, holistic psychology that I am advocating. There were clearly two levels of communication taking place with Jesus, drawing out her own spiritual nature without imposing his own. The fact that a religious concept became part of the conversation (where to worship God) was the result of the therapeutic approach, not the cause of it. Some may even discover that holistic psychology offers a context in which an experience of the Spirit of Jesus can occur, leading to personal faith.

Some will ask, What about sin? Does nonreligious spirituality ignore sin as a cause of much personal disorder? First, sin is a theological term for what otherwise can be described as a distortion of human spirituality. When the apostle Paul describes the effects of sin, he invariably uses social categories rather than individual ones. What he calls "works of the flesh" are basically antisocial forms of behavior—for example, enmity, strife, and jealousy (Gal. 5:20). Sin is not simply a psychological form of pathology. I have discussed sin as a "third dimension" of human spirituality that occurs as a form of inhumanity across the continuum of mental/emotional health and pathology (Anderson, 2002b). Holistic psychology understands the nonreligious aspect of what in theology we call sin. Likewise, holistic psychology as I have presented it can communicate, confer, and affirm in a nonreligious way what in theology we call grace, forgiveness, and even absolution. "If you forgive the sins of any, they are forgiven them" (John 20:23). "Whatever you bind on earth will be bound in heaven, and whatever you loose on earth will be loosed in heaven" (Matt. 18:18). This appears to me to be holistic psychology and practical theology. This is why I want to know more about the person who is driving the car rather than merely being a good mechanic.

Ray S. Anderson is Senior Professor of Theology and Ministry at Fuller Theological Seminary in Pasadena, California, where he has served for 30 years team-teaching integration seminars with faculty from the Graduate School of Psychology. He can be reached at: RAnder9615@aol.com.

References

Anderson, R. S. (2003). *Spiritual caregiving as secular sacrament: A practical theology for professional caregivers*. London: Jessica Kingsley.

Anderson, R. S. (2002a). The social ecology of human personhood: Implications of Dietrich Bonhoeffer's theology for psychology. In T. H. Speidell (Ed.), *On being a person: A multidisciplinary approach to personality theories* (pp. 147-175). Eugene, OR: Wipf and Stock Publishers.

Anderson, R. S. (2002b). Sin: The third dimension of human spirituality. *Christian counseling today, 10*, 26-29.

Anderson, R. S. (1995). *Self-care: A theology of personal empowerment and spiritual healing*. Wheaton, IL: Bridgepoint Books.

Anderson, R. S. (1990). *Christians who counsel—The vocation of holistic therapy*. Grand Rapids, MI: Zondervan.

Anderson, R. S. (1989). Isomorphic indicators in psychological and theological science. *Journal of Psychology and Theology, 17*, 373-381.

Balswick, J. O., King, P. E., Reimer, K. S. (2005). *The reciprocating self: Human development in theological perspective*. Downers Grove, IL: InterVarsity Press.

Barth, K. (1960). *Church dogmatics*, III/2. Edinburgh: T & T Clark.

Becker, E. (1973). *The denial of death*. New York: The Macmillan Company, The Free Press.

Bethge, E. (2000). *Dietrich Bonhoeffer: A biography*. Minneapolis: Fortress Press.

Bonhoeffer, D. (1998). *Sanctorum Communio: A Theological Study of the Sociology of the Church*. Minneapolis: Fortress Press.

Bonhoeffer, D. (1971). *Letters and papers from prison*. New Greatly Enlarged Edition. New York: Macmillan.

Brueggemann, W. (1993). *Biblical perspectives on evangelism: Living in a three-storied universe*. Nashville, TN: Abingdon.

Buber, M. (1970). *I and Thou*. Edinburgh: T. & T. Clark.

Carnell, E. J. (1957). *Christian commitment: An apologetic*, New York: The Macmillan Company.

Carnell, E. J. (1965). *The burden of Søren Kierkegaard*. Grand Rapids, MI: Eerdmans.

Evans, C. S. (1977). *Preserving the person: A look at the human sciences*. Downers Grove, IL: InterVarsity Press.

Evans, C. S. (1988). Healing old wounds and recovering old insights: Toward a Christian view of the person for today. In M. A. Noll & D. F. Wells (Eds.), *Christian faith and practice in the modern world: Theology from an evangelical point of view* (pp. 68-86). Grand Rapids, MI: Eerdmans.

Evans, C. S. (1989). *Wisdom and humanness in psychology: Prospects for a Christian approach*. Grand Rapids, MI: Baker Book House.

Evans, C. S. (1990). *Søren Kierkegaard's Christian psychology*. Grand Rapids, MI: Zondervan.

Evans, C. S. (2006). *Kierkegaard on faith and the self: Collected essays*, Waco, TX: Baylor University Press.

Evans, C. S. (1998). *Faith beyond reason: A Kierkegaardian account*, Grand Rapids: Eerdmans.

Evans, C. S. (1988b). Kierkegaard's view of the unconscious. Paper presented at the International Kierkegaard Symposium, Hillerød, Denmark.

Frankl, V. (1959). *Man's search for meaning: An introduction to logotherapy*, Boston: Beacon Press.

Frankl, V. (1977). *The unconscious God: Psychotherapy and theology*, London: Hodder and Stoughton.

Greenwald, A. G. (1982). Is anyone in charge? Personalysis versus the principle of personal unity. In J. Suls (Ed.) *Psychological perspectives on the self*, Vol. 1 (pp. 151-181). Hillside, NJ; London: Lawrence Erlbaum Associates.

Hunsinger, D. (1995). *Theology and pastoral counseling: A new interdisciplinary approach*. Grand Rapids, MI: Eerdmans Publishing Company.

Kierkegaard, S. (1944). *The concept of dread*. Princeton, NJ: Princeton University Press.

Kierkegaard, S. (1958). *The journals of Søren Kierkegaard*. New York: Harper Torchbooks.

Kierkegaard, S. (1980). *The sickness unto death: A Christian psychological exposition for upbuilding and awakening*. Princeton, NJ: Princeton University Press.

McDonald, G. (1994). *The life God blesses*. Nashville, TN: Thomas Nelson Publishers.

Macmurray, J. (1935). *Reason and emotion*. London: Faber and Faber.

Macmurray, J. (1957). *The self as agent*. London: Faber and Faber, Ltd.

Macmurray, J. (1961). *Persons in relation*. London: Faber and Faber, Ltd.

McFadyen, A. I. (1990). *The call to personhood—A*

Christian theory of the individual in social relationships. New York: Cambridge University Press.

Meissner, W. W. (1987). *Life and faith: Psychological perspectives on religious experience*. Washington, D. C.: Georgetown University Press.

Mowrer, O. H. (1961). *The crisis of psychiatry and religion*. Princeton, NJ: Van Nostrand.

Polanyi, M. (1958). *Personal knowledge*. London: Routledge and Kegan Paul.

Polanyi, M. (1974). *Scientific thought and social reality*. New York: International Universities Press.

Shults, F. L. & S, J. Sandage (2006). *Transforming spirituality: Integrating theology and psychology*, Grand Rapids, MI: Baker Academic.

Torrance, T. (1965). *Theology in reconstruction*. Grand Rapids, MI: Eerdmans.

Tournier, P. (1957). *The meaning of persons*. London: SCM Press.

Young, P. M (1991). *The ontological self in the thinking of C. Stephen Evans and Ray S. Anderson*, unpublished Ph.D. dissertation. Pasadena, CA: Fuller Theological Seminary.

Commentaries on Ray S. Anderson's "Toward a Holistic Psychology: Putting all of the Pieces in their Proper Place"

In conformity with the goals of the Society of Christian Psychology and this journal, a number of commentators were invited to share their "edifying" reactions to the discussion article. Their responses appear below. Ray Anderson then shares his responses to the commentaries in the next article of this special issue of the journal dedicated to his work.

A Holistically Psychological Response to Anderson
Jeffrey P. Bjorck
Fuller Theological Seminary

Ray Anderson has provided a helpful and instructive narrative history regarding the development of his approach to a holistic psychology. I had the honor of co-teaching with him for eight years in a Psychology Integration Seminar at Fuller Theological Seminary. The course covered many of the concepts outlined in Anderson's current article, and I learned much through the process. Among other things, that course focused on his book *Christians Who Counsel* (1990), which included a focus on what he called his "developmental model" of the "integrative self" (p. 32). That model was based in part on the same "wiring diagram" he depicts in his current Figure 1. The following response to Anderson will focus on his "pre-theoretical" model illustrated by his wiring diagram, including commentary regarding what I view as several key strengths. In addition, one modification to the model will be proposed, which might prove especially useful to those with a Calvinistic understanding of original sin and/or psychodynamic psychological inclinations. As a preface to this response, however, comments on Anderson's use of the term "spiritual" will be offered.

Defining Spirituality

Clearly, the terms "spiritual," "religious," "spirituality," and "religiousness" are often used interchangeably in everyday conversation. Conversely, they have also been used to mean different things. Citing Shults and Sandage to this end, Anderson distinguishes between religion as "a multidimensional construct including moral and spiritual practices" and spirituality as "*an experience* [italics added] of transcendence, or the sacred, separate from any established religion" (p. 16). With this in mind, Anderson proposes that Christian psychology is superior to any psychology that does not consider the spiritual aspects of humanity, and he argues for "multilevel competence" (p. 16) as necessary for holistic psychology. This multilevel conceptualization can help Christian psychologists avoid the error of ignoring any aspect of the person, including spirituality. Anderson posits spirituality as a human experience, however, which might be said to emanate from the person as do other dimensions of experience (i.e., mentality, emotionality, physicality, personality). If, however, one considers Jesus' act of breathing on his disciples to convey the Holy Spirit (John 20:22), then spirituality might be said to emanate from God. As such, the question of spirituality can have differing ramifications depending upon whether or not the person in question is one of God's adopted children (Romans 8:15-16). More pointedly, this question will have even greater relevance to the extent that one holds a Calvinistic worldview, including the concept of spiritual death (Calvin & Beveridge, 1990). Such differing perspectives can also impact one's interpretation of Jesus' encounter with the Samaritan woman. For example, Anderson suggested that Jesus' statement regarding her multiple husbands did not embarrass her, but simply prompted a religious question. An alternative interpretation might be that Jesus' pointing to her spiritual sin did convict her and prompted her to try and change the subject via religious debate. As a second example, whereas Anderson suggests that Jesus was "drawing out her own spiritual nature without imposing his own" (p. 14), an alternative view could focus on the fact that Jesus declared his own spiritual nature by saying, "I am He" (John 4:26) before she ever concluded the He was the Christ (John 4:28).

Clearly, the question of how one defines

spirituality will influence how one pursues psychology as a Christian. One's definition of spirituality can also provide a context for an examination of Anderson's holistic model of personhood.

Anderson's Pre-Theoretical Developmental Model of Integrative Personhood

The model of personhood that Anderson depicts in his Figure 1 is most clearly unique in its inclusion of two individuals rather than one. Whereas all models of the self refer to relationships to other persons, Anderson proposes that the "social self" requires another individual in order to exist, for the person cannot be social in isolation. Indeed, elsewhere he has argued that differentiation from other persons is needed for full expression of humans made in the Divine image. Specifically, he noted, "[Kierkegaard's] depiction of the self [as individual] is inadequate to satisfy the biblical account of the self as inherently social, with self-relatedness an ontological construct of the self prior to an existential act of self-reflection" (Anderson, 1995, p. 39). In a 21st century culture that seems to be increasingly individualistic, Anderson's emphasis on the self-as-social is a welcome correction.

I would note, however, that by the time self-reflection is developmentally plausible for the human child, awareness of relations with other persons or even with inanimate objects has already been internalized. Indeed, the foundation of such internalization, Piaget's concept of object permanence (Piaget, cited in Monte, 1980; Ginsburg & Opper, 1988), has recently been documented in infants as young as 2.5 months of age to a limited extent (Aguiar & Baillargeon, 1999). Hence, I would propose that the individual does not need others always physically present to remain a social self. Moreover, I would suggest that the individual does not need others present to maintain relationship with God, which was aptly demonstrated by John Bunyan, who created his *Pilgrim's Progress* while incarcerated in isolation (Brown, 1928).

As such, social relatedness—while essential for the full expression of the human person—can be viewed as secondary in priority to the person's relationship with God, which itself can be construed as interpersonal in the ultimate sense. Whereas Genesis states that it was not good for Adam to be alone, Adam's relationship with God was to take precedence over his relationship with Eve. In choosing to place Eve's desires over God's by taking the fruit she offered, Adam sinned. This observation notwithstanding, Anderson's emphasis on the social self still stands as a clear strength of his model and it points to the need of community for the full expression of the image of God in persons pursuing wholeness.

A second strength of Anderson's model involves the emphasis on spirituality as involving all other dimensions of the person, consisting of "an orientation to God as Spirit which runs right back through each of the other subsets or subsystems of the self." One reason for the strength of this aspect of the model is not stated in Anderson's current article, but can be found in one of his earlier works (Anderson, 1990). Seeing the spiritual as being experienced (versus existing) last developmentally and then coursing back through all other dimensions of self prevents the illusion that one could be truly spiritually healthy without attending to all facets of the self. As Anderson explains, "If the spiritual dimension of selfhood was portrayed as the first or highest in the model, this could lead to the assumption that one could develop a spiritual life and orientation toward God with no real integration of the other aspects of the self, or even with a neglect of these aspects" (1990. p. 35). In his current essay, Anderson illustrates this problem well via his reference to Kierkegaard's self-admitted failure to marry Regina Olsen. Conversely, however, it seems important to note that Anderson's conception of the spirit as "an orientation to God" does not address the question of how this orientation is influenced by salvation. One might infer that a non-Christian's spiritual subsystem would be considered to be impaired, but this is not completely clear, and Christians can also presumably have impairments in the spiritual realm. Thus, additional clarity in the model would be helpful here.

A third strength, related to the second, is Anderson's emphases on balance (e.g., between mental and physical, among the five subsystems, and between individuality and sociality). The 21st century culture, in addition to being individualistic, is also increasingly compartmentalized. As such, Anderson's emphasis on holistic living is refreshingly countercultural. Indeed, as noted elsewhere, I would propose that a reasonable rephrase of Jesus' greatest commandment (Mark 12:30) is, "Love the Lord your God with your whole person, with your whole person, with your whole person, and with your whole person" (Bjorck, 2007a, p. 57). As such, Anderson points to the value of the human life lived in balance, without neglect of, or undue focus on, any aspect of personhood.

One modification of Anderson's developmental model could come in the form of an additional subsystem experienced prior to all others. Of course, suggesting that it would precede all other subsystems must be qualified by Anderson's describing his model as a "spiral staircase" and not a strictly linear progression. Having said this, I propose a *pre-social* subsystem preceding all other subsystems, involving the experience of self-as-all. Whereas Anderson is correct that social context is indeed the infant's first reality, I would emphasize that it is a reality of which the infant is initially unaware. Rather, as Sullivan (1953) has proposed, I consider the infant's earliest experience to be "prototaxic" (p. 75). Prototaxic experience does not differentiate self from others, nor does it incorporate temporal awareness. Piaget, whose work informed Sullivan's, theorized that this developmental period involved *"feelings of efficacy* in the sense that the infant believes that his *desires* are responsible for the presence of [stimuli, e.g., food]" (Monte, 1980, p. 351). Moreover, the infant's "existence is everything that exists, for without *his* immediate perception of objects, there simply are none" (Monte, p. 351).

Including a pre-social subsystem enables the identification of original sin, manifested by the continued unconscious desire to experience oneself as all-powerful and self-sufficient (i.e., self-as-all). Elsewhere (Bjorck, 2007c), I have described how this irrational desire can be inferred from illusions of control (Bjorck & Rogers, 2005; Rogers & Bjorck, 2004), which are a normative aspect of human experience. Simply identifying this desire for self-sufficiency and/or control illusions, however, may not eliminate them, in light of their proposed infantile origins in the *pre-social* subsystem. Given that the inception of this subsystem is proposed as predating logical reasoning, its continuance in defiance of logical reality is understandable. Thus, for example, a parent whose two children have conflicting performances (e.g., a ball game and a piano recital) may feel irrationally guilty for only attending one or the other, rather than logically sad regarding her inability to be two places at once. As another example, a person accosted by an armed gunman may find himself feeling irrationally ashamed for failing to disarm the assailant (Bjorck, 2007b). A third example is provided by the psychodynamic concept of *resistance* to change (Monte, 1980), which is so typically seen in psychotherapy. Whereas clients consciously wish to remediate their respective situations, the unconscious desire to remain the same is also often observed. I would propose that this phenomenon is a manifestation of the originally sinful desire to perceive self as sufficient, in need of no alterations. As such, the concept of change would threaten the unconscious pre-social self-as-all, resulting in resistance.

In summary, adding a *pre-social* subsystem to Anderson's model provides the means for explaining how the good image of God can be tainted by original sin within the context of personhood. Such a subsystem, like all others in Anderson's spiral staircase, would have the potential to be experienced at various points in development and would help to explain unconscious resistance to healthy change, as well as conscious choices to do wrong in spite of also having the desire to do what is right (Romans 7).

Conclusion

Anderson's proposal for a holistic psychology provides the Christian psychologist, or the psychologist who is a Christian, with an extremely useful framework for conceptualizing and interacting with persons made in the image of God. The concept of integration as a personal quality of whole persons has clear advantages over integration as the relegation of religiousness to a sub-domain of psychological study. Moreover, viewing spirituality as a core dimension, free of religious trappings, is also useful when considering persons of any faith worldview (including atheism). Framing the spiritual subsystem in this way, however, may also involve risk. Whereas defining spirituality as nonreligious can avoid doctrinal constraints and can permit the psychologist to view all persons as spiritual, this definition also creates ambiguity regarding any potential differences between spiritual concerns for Christians versus non-Christians. This will likely be more of a concern for those with Calvinistic leanings regarding the spiritual death of unregenerate persons, but others might also question how Anderson's model distinguishes what is unique regarding those who are Christian believers. Even with this caveat, Anderson's model has many strengths. In particular, his emphases on the self-as-social, the self-as-spiritual, and the healthy self-as-balanced all provide helpful parameters for those wishing to be intentional as Christian psychologists who serve in a nonreligious context with spiritual integrity.

Jeff Bjorck, Ph.D., is Professor of Psychology at Fuller Theological Seminary; Graduate School of Psychology; 180 N. Madison Avenue; Pasadena, CA 91101. His email address is. jbjorck@fuller.edu.

References

Aguiar, A., & Baillargeon, R. (1999). 2.5-month-old infants' reasoning about when objects should and should not be occluded. *Cognitive Psychology, 39*, 116-157.

Anderson, R. S. (1990). *Christians who counsel: The vocation of wholistic therapy*. Grand Rapids, MI: Zondervan.

Anderson, R. S. (1995). *Self Care: A theology of personal empowerment and spiritual healing*. Wheaton, IL: Victor Books.

Bjorck, J. P. (2007a). Autobiographical reflections on psychology and the artistic spirit. *Journal of Psychology and Christianity, 26*, 57-60.

Bjorck, J. P. (2007b). A Christian Application of Multimodal Therapy. *Journal of Psychology and Christianity, 26*, 140-150.

Bjorck, J. P. (2007c). Faith, coping, and illusory control: Psychological constructs with theological ramifications. *Journal of Psychology and Christianity, 26*, 195-206.

Bjorck, J. P., & Rogers, S.A. (2005). *Religiousness and illusory control in the face of stress*. Paper presented at the 113th Annual Convention of the American Psychological Association, Washington, DC.

Calvin, J., & Beveridge, H. (1990). *Institutes of the Christian religion (two volumes in one)*. Grand Rapids, MI: Wm. B. Eerdmans Publishing Company.

Brown, J. (1928). *John Bunyan (1628-1688): His life, times, and work*. London, England: The Hulbert Publishing Company.

Ginsburg, H. P., & Opper, S. (1988). *Piaget's theory of intellectual development, 3rd Edition*. Englewood Cliffs, NJ: Prentice Hall.

Monte, C. F. (1980). *Beneath the mask: An introduction to theories of personality*. New York, NY: Holt, Rinehart, and Winston.

Rogers, S. A., & Bjorck, J. P. (2004). *Illusory control and unrealistic optimism on persistence amidst failure*. Poster presented at the 112th Annual Convention of the American Psychological Association, Honolulu, HI.

Sullivan, H. S. (1953). *The interpersonal theory of psychiatry*. New York, NY: W. W. Norton and Company.

Response to Anderson's "Toward a Holistic Psychology"
Don Browning
University of Chicago, Emeritus

I am in almost complete agreement with the case that Ray Anderson has set forth for a holistic psychology. I will try to show why this is so and then suggest ways to argue his position in a slightly different form. I propose this rephrasing of his point of view for the possible advantages it might provide in negotiating the complex terrain of professional psychology, theology, culture, and the life of the church.

To say it directly and simply, I think, Anderson is searching for a thick or multidimensional pre-empirical view of human action. He is proposing a model of human action that brings the spiritual directly into our view of the self – a view of the self that could guide both psychological research and practice. It also should be a model formally adequate for the description of personhood in the Christian faith and, indeed, most other religions as well. It is, as Anderson suggests, a nonreligious model that is adequate to a variety of spiritualities in contrast to one specific religious tradition and its institutional forms. Anderson believes that a horizon of spirituality essentially qualifies or helps define the self. Spirituality is not something added on to the human psychological self, as psychologists often think about it. Nor is it something that emerges in the self only as a kind of leap when one is driven to the depth of despair or "dread," as Kierkegaard thought. Spirituality, he contends, is a defining element of one's relationship to others in a community of shared values and meaning. Anderson believes spirituality reaches down into the self and shapes one's inner psychological reactions, emotions, sexuality, and physical life. In searching for his model, Anderson works his way through Kierkegaard, Stephen Evans, John Macmurray, and finally arrives at the model of the self in Dietrich Bonhoeffer. Bonhoeffer saw the self as emerging from the community. The spirituality of the self emerges when the recognition and formation of the community becomes objectified as a "third" – a kind of dialectic, as I understand it, between individual intentionality and the response of the community (the "Other" in community) - that is then internalized into a stable structure of the self. Depending on the kind of spirituality in question, the God of Christianity, or some other form of the sacred can be a dimension of this communal Other and then become a settled yet dynamic structure of the self. Anderson believes that psychologists need to take account of the spiritual aspect of the self in both their research and their therapeutic interventions.

Anderson is looking for what I call a pre-empirical view of human action that would require psychology to include the spiritual in all that it does. I would not call it a "pre-theoretical" view, as Anderson does. It seems to me that it is theoretical through and through and, very good theory at that. But it is pre-empirical; it is the kind of work psychologists have to do time and again when they are empirically studying a field of human behavior, whether it be morality, virtue, health, love, forgiveness, or hope. As Lawrence Kohlberg (1981, p. 134) turned to Plato and Kant for his pre-empirical theory of morality to guide his empirical research in moral psychology, Anderson is searching for an adequate pre-empirical model of self and action to capture the dimension of spirituality for the whole of psychology. Terry Cooper and I do much the same thing in the second edition of *Religious Thought and the Modern Psychologies* (Browning & Cooper, 2004). I do it even more explicitly in my recent *Christian Ethics and the Moral Psychologies* (Browning, 2006).

Here is how I talk in a somewhat different way about some of the concerns that Anderson has. Although I am a practical theologian and theological ethicist, when I address the academic discipline of psychology, I distance myself a bit from my theological beginning point and speak more phenomenologically. Here I often say, as does Anderson, that much of psychology has a too narrow view of human action and selfhood. This narrowness damages, skews, and renders reductionistic much of psychology's research and interventions. Increasingly, using hermeneutic models of human action found in Hans-Georg Gadamer and especially Paul Ricoeur, I get some of the same insights that Anderson derives from Macmurray and Bonhoeffer. But my model sounds a little different. I speak more of humans as creatures of *phronesis* or practical wisdom. This is something like Macmurray's "practical agent." I further argue, following Gadamer and Ricoeur, that humans are active practical actors and interpreters of how community and tradition shape their individual selves.

But in reading Ricoeur carefully, I factor out five dimensions of human action that an adequate psychology should assume and study: 1) a practice dimension made up of internalizations in the self of inherited communal patterns; 2) a teleological or desiring dimension through which we seek to meet our human needs in and through our communally shaped practices; 3) a narrative dimension shaped by communities of tradition that tell us about the meaning of life and our place in it; 4) a moral dimension that gives us general principles of obligation; and 5) more prudential strategies for working these prior dimensions into context-specific concrete action. This, from my perspective, is an alternative way of conceptualizing a pre-empirical theory of human action and self that accomplishes some of the objectives of Anderson's model.

When I speak phenomenologically to psychologists (even though I am a theologian), I often chide them for leaving out one or more of the dimensions in their understanding of persons. I would agree with Anderson that they habitually omit the spiritual. In describing the spiritual, I would, when speaking to the psychologist, make fewer references to God as the core of the spiritual than does Anderson. But I would use the word "sacred" since it covers a wider range of spiritualities; the word God is so closely associated with the Abrahamic religions.

For me, the spiritual dimension of the self is best found in the narrative dimension of my five levels listed above. All people carry in their selves broad narratives about the meaning of life. I follow Gadamer in believing that these narratives are shaped by what he calls our "effective history" – the way past traditions mediated by surrounding communities pass along to us their elaborations of the meaning of human existence. This effective history is part of our human experience even if we cannot consciously identify it or even clearly interpret its meaning. It is communally mediated and always contains horizons defining the ultimate context of experience as a particular tradition has defined it. In the case of Christianity, which indeed informs the pre-reflective experience of most people in western societies, this narratively represented horizon of sacrality may be defined with reference to acts of God as conceived by Jews and Christians down through the ages.

This view of the spiritual self is a bit more phenomenologically and historically weighted than I sense in Anderson. To understand the spirituality of the self, the psychologist must perform an act of hermeneutical interpretation of not only the narrative identity of the subject but also that of her internalized images of parents, family lines, surrounding communities, and explicit communities of faith. To me, the best psychology of spirituality (or "psychology of faith," as Anderson sometimes calls it) can be found in the clinical and psycho-historical studies of Erik Erikson – especially his studies of Luther and Gandhi (Erikson, 1958, 1969).

Anderson and I agree that the spiritual dimension defines the self to its core. In my language, this means that the narrative horizon shapes the other four dimensions – our everyday practices and habits, our needs and desires, our moral sense, and our practical strategies in particular contexts. However true this is, it is important to allow psychologists to use a differentiated view of the self to guide their research and therapeutic interventions. Our spiritual narratives and communal effective histories should not be allowed to trump or totally control in psychological research the other dimensions of action - our practices, needs and desires, moral cognitions, and practical strategies. Our spiritually freighted narratives influence and shape these other dimensions, sometimes decisively but at other times only slightly. We may all be people of faith, relying to some degree on the communal spiritualities of the past. Our faith, however, may be weak, confused, poorly informed, and inadequately tested. We must permit the psychologist to gain some *distance* (in contrast to a totally disregarding objectivity) from the narratively shaped spirituality of the self in order to study empirically our habits, needs, emotions, moral cognitions, and practical strategies in their more differentiated states.

At the same time that I would urge Anderson to take a more phenomenological tone when trying to convince both secular and Christian psychologists to widen their theories of human action and selfhood. I also would not hesitate to remove the brackets of phenomenology and assume the mantle of the theologian once again. I readily do this in my writings to critique the relative adequacy – theologically, ethically, and philosophically – of the implicit spiritualities buried in many psychological and psychotherapeutic systems. Psychology can simultaneously easily ignore the spiritual and yet unwittingly invent a variety of alternative spiritualities. Unearthing these hidden spiritualities in the modern psychologies has been an explicit interest of mine over the years just as it has been for Ray Anderson. (I first attempted to do this in my *Generative Man* [Browning, 1973], and later in *Religious Thought and the Modern Psychologies* [Browning & Cooper, 2004] and in *Christian Ethics and the Moral Psychologies* [Browning, 2006].) It is one thing to speak phenomenologically to psychologists in order to get them to broaden their models of the self. It is another thing, and an entirely honorable thing, for theologians to review the relative adequacy of various psychologies from a theological point of view. Both of these are important tasks. Although this fine essay is a contribution primarily to the first endeavor, it puts Anderson in an excellent position to continue his contributions to the second.

Don Browning is Alexander Campbell Professor Emeritus of Ethics and the Social Sciences in the Divinity School. His address is Swift Hall 401, 1025 E. 58th St., Chicago, IL 60637. The email address is dsbrowni@midway.uchicago.edu.

References

Browning, D. (2006). *Christian ethics and the moral psychologies*. Grand Rapids, MI: Wm. B. Eerdmans.

Browning, D. (1973). *Generative Man*. Louisville, KY: Westminster John Knox.

Browning, D., & Cooper, T. (2004). *Religious thought and the modern psychologies*. Minneapolis, MN: Fortress Press.

Erikson, E. (1958). *Young Man Luther*. New York: W.W. Norton.

Erikson, E. (1969). *Gandhi's Truth*. New York: W.W. Norton.

Kohlberg, L. (1981). *The philosophy of moral development*. New York: Harper and Row.

A Winning Hand? Reflections on Ray Anderson's "Toward a Holistic Psychology"

Trey Buchanan
Wheaton College

Not unlike a gambler's bold move to beat the house, Ray Anderson's description of a new foundation for Christian psychology lays everything on the line in favor of a thoroughly robust, coherent, and spiritual conception of personhood. His description directly challenges what he sees as the losing hands of reductionism, positivism, and methodology that have consistently plagued the field of integration. But are those of us committed to the task of integration willing to place our bet on his "coherent construal" of personhood that promises not just a better Christian psychology, but also a broader-reaching "nonreligious Christian psychology" that trumps all others?

Upon considering Anderson's essay, I find myself deeply aware of two issues at stake in this bold move. The first is relevance. By not reaching for a new, multifaceted conception of personhood grounded in spirituality, the progress of integration will continue to be as thin as the view of personhood it often appropriates from either contemporary scientific psychology or the wider culture of academia. Scholars and practitioners have been in pursuit of a compelling Christian psychology for decades with what seems to be little progress beyond the establishment of relatively insular conversation, one that rarely gets noticed by mainstream psychology. Without the kind of vision Anderson puts forth, Christian psychology may just continue existing as only a footnote in the history of psychology and religion.

The second issue at stake is truth. By this I mean that Anderson's holistic psychology of personhood is grounded in the belief that it represents a truer conception of what it means to be human than all other conceptions. This high epistemological status is derived from Anderson's consistent reminder that spirituality lies at the center of all that we are and all that we experience. Spirituality connects us not only to God and the world he created, but more importantly, it connects us to ourselves. Opposed to integrating psychology with theology, he saturates psychology with spirituality. Ultimately this spiritual primacy provides Anderson's personhood with the coherence, consistency, and holism that he sees as the warrant for its truth.

The upside of the Anderson's holistic conception of personhood is quite enticing. By following his lead, we just might live to see a paradigm shift from the mere integration of two scholarly fields to a robust and influential Christian psychology that would radically transform the science and practice of psychology. Echoing the imagery of Jesus' Sermon on the Mount, the promise of a Christian psychology will no longer be hidden but be allowed to shine for God's glory.

However, is there a downside to Anderson's bold move? While it might be argued that there really is nothing to lose by such a gamble, I fear Anderson's essay does hold a weak card, one that may ultimately limit its success.

This weakness is his presentation of the scientific nature of psychology and its contributions to his conception of personhood. In the initial paragraph of his essay, Anderson claims his holistic psychology is "derived from a scientific understanding of 'whole persons;'" such as science, as he describes later, "develops its knowledge base out of actual observation and participation in the life experience of others, not least of all its therapeutic experience." As one follows Anderson's description of the various pieces of his concept of personhood, no connections are made to the vast and diverse findings of over a century's worth of empirical research in psychology. Further, while collection of teachers and writers from which he constructs his view of the person include profoundly influential individuals, they are neither scientists nor psychologists, but theologians and philosophers. From how it is presented in this essay, being "scientific" seems to mean merely living with others and observing them, especially in their suffering and healing. There is no doubt that this provides valuable and profound insights into what it means to be human; it should be construed as either science or scientific.

Thus the approach taken in this essay is not an alternative to the dichotomization of science and religion, but actually one that perpetuates their separation by not benefiting from a thorough engagement with mainstream psychological science. His brief descriptions of physicality beg to be fleshed out by the findings of contemporary neuroscience, recent advances in cultural psychology could ground his argument for a shared human spirituality, and the new field of positive psychology surely echoes his call for a holistic conception of human flourishing. More specifically, his description of development of the person rests upon psychological conceptions of infants and young children that have no empirical support – for over the past 25 years, developmental psychologists have provided evidence that standard theories grossly underestimate the cognitive and emotional capacities of infants. Any conception of persons that is to be compelling and, I feel, ultimately true, cannot afford to miss the opportunity to engage with the findings and methods of a recognizable scientific psychology.

This commentary's praise and criticism together stress the importance of engaging directly with the fields of contemporary psychological science, by both the community of self-identified Christian psychologists and the various stripes of Christians-who-are-psychologists with whom they share common cause.

Trey Buchanan is Associate Professor of Psychology Undergraduate Coordinator with the Department of Psychology, Wheaton College, Wheaton, IL 60187. His email address is trey.buchanan@wheaton.edu

---

Toward a Holistic Psychology: Enriching the Puzzle – a Perichoretic Response
Graham Buxton
Tabor College, Adelaide

In reflecting on Ray Anderson's metaphor of pieces of a puzzle in his pre-theoretical model of personhood, I am reminded of some well-known words from a poem by rabbi Lawrence Kushner (1977) in *Honey from the Rock*, cited by Anderson (2001) in *The New Age of Soul*:

> Each lifetime is the pieces of a jigsaw puzzle.
> For some there are more pieces.
> For others the puzzle is more difficult to assemble …
>
> But know this. No one has within themselves
> All the pieces to their puzzle …
>
> Everyone carries with them at least one and probably
> Many pieces to someone else's puzzle.

So, quoting Macmurray, "I need you to be myself." The two core theses in Anderson's paper are (1) theology and psychology are not dichotomous fields of study in need of integration, but two disciplines that derive from the same spiritual stem and, as a consequence, natural conversation partners; and (2) the affirmation that "we cannot experience true subjectivity apart from the encounter and relation with other subjects." In other words, our essential identity as human beings is grounded in the fact that we are, in the words of Douglas John Hall (1986, p. 116) 'Being-With' creatures, in which self-transcendence, mutuality and reciprocity – in *active movements* towards the (human) Other – ontologically define personal subjectivity. Anderson draws selectively, but deeply, from the wells of philosophical anthropology, psychology, and theology in expounding his holistic psychology of human personhood.

I am indebted to the concepts put forward by Anderson. They confront the selfism and individualism so prevalent in post-Enlightenment thinking with regard to human personhood. However, I would like to highlight in this necessarily brief response two additions to Anderson's schematic proposal that I hope will serve to enrich the puzzle that he is assembling. The first has to do with the innertrinitarian doctrine of *perichoresis*, on which human identity and community is theologically predicated, a doctrine that speaks into the dynamic relationality that lies at the core of human personhood. The second area derives from an appreciation of Jürgen Moltmann's notion of "creation-community," taking us beyond personal relations as an essentialist framework for *imago Dei*. These two ideas are related, since *perichoresis* is an appropriate construct for interpreting human existence within the dynamic order of God's creation-community.

Perichoresis is a Greek word that refers to the intense mutual indwelling within the life of the Trinity. It is an inclusive concept that directs us into the essential nature of God's inner being of community and dynamic relationality, whose energies are not contained within his innertrinitarian being, but spill out in other-centered love to all creation. Paul Fiddes points out that Thomas Aquinas' Trinitarian conception emphasizes movements or actions within God rather than subjects who act in various ways, which leads Fiddes (2000, pp. 71-81) to propose a *perichoresis* of movements rather than a *perichoresis* of divine subjects in his Trinitarian ontology. This perspective is theologically permissible, of course, so long as we hold that ontology and relationality are neither separate nor opposite, but complementary.

In this scenario God may be described as "an event of relationships," a phrase that echoes the agency and active movement implicit in Macmurray's personalist philosophy. Whilst we cannot sustain a direct correspondence between the perichoretic interiority of the divine persons and human sociality (Volf, 1998, p. 211), we may propose a modified form of *perichoresis* in the experience of active reciprocity and resistance that lie at the heart of human relationships, an idea that I develop more fully in *The Trinity, Creation and Pastoral Ministry* (Buxton, 2005). This line of thought is helpful in articulating a holistic psychology of human personhood – or, in Anderson's words, a "non-religious Christian psychology" – because it reinforces the notion that we are essentially "spiritual beings having a human experience" (Chardin). In our mutual giving and receiving, "we participate in a sort of availability analogous to that which the Trinitarian persons enjoy for one another" (Rogers, 2001, p. 271). To introduce the language of *perichoresis* with regard to human personhood is, therefore, to propose a relational spirituality that is first and foremost *human* and not religious.

The Trinitarian concept of perichoresis is in fact helpful at a number of levels of reality. In addition to its theological, social, and pastoral significance, the concept correlates scientifically with an understanding of the interconnectedness of all creation in a coherent, open-ended and complex system of reality. This cosmic perspective finds fruitful expression in Moltmann's (2000, p. 117) notion of a "creation-community," a community of both creatures and environments contributing to a "web of life on earth" that is grounded in an inclusive Trinity that is "so wide open that the whole world can find room and rest and eternal life within it."

An increasingly pivotal affirmation in theological anthropology is that human beings have been created for relationship not just with God and with each other, but also with the physical creation. Tillich's ontology of existence, for example, is profoundly rich in its insistence that to be created *imago Dei* takes us beyond the experience of I-Thou personal encounter with God – and each other – into an awareness that we are embraced by a transcendent power of being in which *all things* participate: "the self is only self because it has a world, a structured universe, to which it belongs and from which it is separated at the same time" (Tillich, 1952, p. 90). The emerging discipline of science-and-religion offers similar insights. So human beings are summoned to participate intimately and adventurously in God's good and holy creation precisely because they are thereby enabled to discover the richness of human life in all its intensity and depth.

Human self-identity is therefore contingent upon openness to the created order, both human and non-human, and not just to other persons, taking us beyond Macmurray's personalist exposition of Other. To the integrating concept of sociality, therefore, we need to add a more generous appreciation of the symbiotic relationship between human beings and the natural order of things: as dust of the earth, human beings are not only in continuity with nature: they are in *communion* with nature. The history of the world is the history of nature being summoned by the Spirit to *be itself* as a gloriously diverse and perichoretic reality, even as human beings are being summoned by the same Spirit to discover *their true selves* in relationship with each other, with the world of nature, and with the triune God who has brought all things into being.

A truly authentic holistic psychology of personhood, therefore, requires the incorporation of both a divinely-ordained perichoretic structure and a robust ecological dimension as additional integrative components of Anderson's pre-theoretical schematic "wiring diagram." These two elements are in continuity with his underlying relational model of personhood predicated on a spiritual core that is non-religious, though capable of full religious expression.

Graham Buxton is Director of Postgraduate Studies in Ministry and Theology at Tabor College, Adelaide, Australia. He can be reached at: buxton@aapt.net.au.

References

Anderson, R. S. (2001). *The new age of soul: Spiritual wisdom for a new millennium*. Eugene, OR: Wipf and Stock.

Buxton, G. (2005). *The Trinity, creation and pastoral ministry: Imaging the perichoretic God* (pp. 167-176). Milton Keynes: Paternoster.

Fiddes, P. S. (2000). *Participating in God: A pastoral doctrine of the Trinity* (pp. 71-81). London: Darton, Longman & Todd.

Hall, D. J. (1986). *Imaging God: Dominion as stewardship*. Grand Rapids: Eerdmans.

Kushner, L. (1977). *Honey from the rock: Visions of Jewish mystical renewal*. New York: Harper & Row.

Moltmann, J. (2000). Perichoresis: An old magic word for a new trinitarian theology. In M. D. Meeks (Ed.), *Trinity, community, and power: Mapping trajectories in Wesleyan theology*. Nashville: Kingswood Books.

Rogers, E. F. Jr. (2001). The stranger as blessing. In J. J. Buckley, & D. S. Yeago (Eds.), *Knowing the triune God: The work of the Spirit in the practices of the church*. Grand Rapids: Eerdmans.

Tillich, P. (1952). *The courage to be*. London: Collins Fontana.

Volf, M. (1998). *After our likeness: The church as the image of the Trinity*. Grand Rapids: Eerdmans.

A Few Thoughts on the Applied Side of Anderson's Holistic Psychology

Marv Erisman
Azusa Pacific University

In this brief response, I would like to focus on the practical and applied idea of holistic psychology. First of all, however, I would like to acknowledge the contribution Anderson has made to the field of integration. His essay clearly identifies the rich complexity of his lifetime, conversational partners and the sources of his thinking. The emphasis on the social nature of personhood and his underlying appreciation for the phenomenological stance bring pragmatic value to the conversation surrounding integration. His desire to move integration beyond a narrow interaction of perspectives between theology and psychology is critical if we are to train and educate psychotherapists who, within their Christian traditions, can actually *practice* integrative psychotherapy within the urban, pluralistic landscape. Integrative psychotherapy, however it is conceptualized, must have the capacity to be equally relevant and helpful with clients from every walk of life. Otherwise, our academic conversations, though meaningful and contributory to the evolution of our understanding of integration, will practically impact only a few.

Conceptual models of integration need feet that carry them into the therapy room. Within the past decade the gate has been opened to incorporate spirituality into the psychotherapeutic conversation through the increased appreciation for diversity within our professional associations. Though still controversial in some clinics and treatment centers, (even those whose mission is explicitly Christian), as reported by trainees and interns, attending to spirituality is now firmly rooted in the literature and within the professional associations. Anderson's holistic psychology provides a conceptual frame for the applied work of psychotherapy. His understanding of social reality as spiritual in its core and his practical emphasis on non-religious spirituality are most helpful for the practice of integration within a secular, urban, and pluralistic world. His holistic psychology, however, might be strengthened by a few additional perspectives – perspectives that are not foreign to him, yet are not explicitly connected to his holistic psychology as outlined in this article. These perspectives are offered not as criticisms of his work, but as reflections along our mutual journey of *practiced* integration.

The work of psychotherapy is essentially the unpacking of our embedded, relational world. Psychotherapy is a "breakthrough" exercise, an attempt to help us understand our individual narrative from within our social context. It is an attempt to explore our story with its rich texture of challenges and struggles. This unpacking is often painful. Our discoveries confront us with the dark side of individual freedom, with choices that hurt and injure, and with the limiting beliefs and values that create barriers to our emerging personhood as we explore the fullness of our belonging with others. The hope, nevertheless, is that through the psychotherapeutic encounter we will break through our negative, embedded narrative and intentionally construct a "new" place for ourselves in our same old world.

By positing the belief that social reality is spiritual at its core, Anderson acknowledges the transcendent nature of historical and social reality (see also Niebuhr, 1964). He legitimizes the place of the spiritual within the psychotherapeutic dialogue and in the exercise of unpacking our narratives. It is helpful also, as he does, to separate the spiritual from the religious and theological. By doing so, the therapeutic conversation remains more open to individual meaning-making along three connected but separable lines of inquiry.

Yet most of us either inherit or enjoin a community of interpretation regarding the spiritual (Walsh, 1999; Griffith & Griffith, 2002). This interpretation of the spiritual is often contained within our families, and certainly within our religious communities, religious practices, and theological beliefs. Individual spirituality is rarely "pure," or in a primary manner disconnected from this interpretation, but rather, often "contaminated" with beliefs, values, and practices that add confusion to our narratives and our sense-making. The God who is good becomes the bad object; the community of faith becomes a source of guilt and shaming; and the parents who desire to create upright, spiritual character in their children become tightly wound religionists, and so on. Integrative psychotherapy must unpack this material. When it does, the non-religious spirituality as grounded in our social reality may fade in significance to the hard work of deconstructing and reconstructing the individual narrative. The fluid and dynamic beliefs and values that swirl around our developing personhood often create our barriers of engagement with God and with each other. When spirituality appears too disconnected from religious and theological material, that itself might need unpacking.

During the past decade, as the gates opened to "permit" the dialogue of spirituality into the therapeutic hour, those teaching integration celebrated and felt vindicated. It was, after all, long overdue. Our social narratives had always contained our spiritual journeys, and our mental models were finally deconstructed to more closely match the lived reality of our individual and social lives. This enlightened attitude has, however, created an imbalance. By focusing our attention on the critical nature of spirituality, we have relegated the moral landscape of our social interaction to the status of a distant cousin. Social reality is both spiritual and moral at its core in the non-religious sense that Anderson suggests. Our social narrative is an admixture of the spiritual and moral. It reflects both types of intentional, social engagement (Walsh, 1999). The beliefs and values that define our spirituality and moral perspectives may be disconnected from any religious or theological language, or they might be connected in interesting, and sometimes disturbing ways. The spiritual and moral dimensions have equal metaphoric capacity to define the lived reality of our personhood. and consequently both might need to be unpacked during the psychotherapeutic dialogue. To forget this or to subsume the moral under the religious is a reductionism equal to the reductionism practiced for decades within psychotherapy as regards to the spiritual (Doherty, 1995).

Anderson's holistic psychotherapy is grounded in a biblical anthropology, one in which God is so fundamentally central to the social narrative that he is in some sense disengaged from it. Yet it is with God's permission, or so it seems, that we work out our social reality without His direct involvement. This, at least, seems to be Bonhoeffer's logic as outlined by Anderson. This understanding does provide a refreshing and liberating starting point for the psychotherapist. It removes the trappings of an engaged God who is somehow responsible for all our troubles and sufferings, and opens the door to full accountability for individual choices and behavior. Individual sense-making during the therapeutic hour with regard to spirituality is granted a wide swath within this viewpoint. The obvious danger, however, is the metaphoric disconnection of God from spirituality. Though this may sound odd, the social reality with spirituality at its core, that non-religious spirituality that underlies our social being, might ironically devolve into an individual's closet construction of idiosyncratic spirituality with no significant object, except oneself, as a point of reference. Since, as Husserl (1967) pointed out, all consciousness is "consciousness of," that is, it is intentional and has an object, how does an integrative psychotherapy celebrate non-religious spirituality without becoming so open-minded that individual spirituality trumps the social narrative and ironically sustains an unwanted individual liminality?

Social reality is defined by our human freedom. Human freedom is at the heart of a biblical anthropology. Anderson's holistic psychology with its emphasis on non-religious spirituality underscores the central role of individual freedom. To live before God, but without God, introduces an "as if" that places the burden of our social narrative and the becoming of our personhood squarely on our mutual, communal shoulders. Our freedom, and more specifically our choices, becomes the stacking effect of our individual and social identity. The God who is constantly present, yet permits us to work out our salvation within the structure of our social reality, seems sadly, in a practical way disinterested (if I interpret this correctly). Freedom, in a practical and conceptual way, seems more psychotherapeutically helpful, and perhaps more biblically grounded if it is viewed as part of the intentional nature of consciousness. Then our choices, for good or ill, within the structure of our freedom, are made with God as partner and as presence. God's transcendence is an interpreted transcendence – that is also part of our freedom, for good or ill. It also needs our exercise of unpacking.

Reinhold Niebuhr's (1964) definition of sin as the misuse of freedom is an excellent example of a definitional framework that provides clarity within the paradigm of a non-religious spirituality. The brokenness of our social relations is easily understood when sin is defined in this manner, regardless of our religious backgrounds. We need more definitions like this one that provide psychotherapists with theological language and vocabulary that supports the exploration of spirituality and morality within the therapeutic encounter.

Marv Erisman is Professor of Psychology and Director of Interdisciplinary Integration, Department of Graduate Psychology, Azusa Pacific University. He may be reached at merisman@apu.edu.

References

Doherty, W. (1995). *Soul searching: why psychotherapy must promote moral responsibility*. New York, NY: Basic Books.

Griffith, J.L. & Griffith, M.E. (2002). *Encountering the sacred in psychotherapy*. New York: The Guilford Press.

Husserl, E. (1967). *Phenomenology*. New York: Anchor Books Doubleday & Company.

Niebuhr, R. (1964). *The Nature and Destiny of Man*. New York: Charles Scribner's Sons.

Walsh, F. (Ed.). (1999). *Spiritual resources in family therapy*. New York: The Guilford Press.

Anderson's Encounter with Kierkegaard

C. Stephen Evans
Baylor University

I appreciate Ray Anderson's attempt to sketch a holistic account of psychology. Anderson's account has many virtues. I think he is profoundly right to emphasize the relational character of the human selves as meaning-seeking beings, both ontologically and ethically. His view also rightly avoids any kind of social reductionism that would deny agency and responsibility to the individual. In the end, I think his view is very close to the kind of view I would defend myself, one that sees humans as having a spiritual core that is rightly filled by a relation to the Creator, but that can be exercised in ways that, on the surface at least, look non-religious.

I also appreciate the careful and sympathetic attention Anderson has paid to Kierkegaard and to my own work on Kierkegaard, as well as my work in developing a philosophy of the person. I would like to respond to one gentle criticism he makes. If I understand him rightly, he thinks my interpretation of Kierkegaard is overly charitable, in that I read Kierkegaard as more of a relational thinker than he is. I try to make Kierkegaard less of an individualist than he is by seeing relations with others, including relations with other humans, as part of the ontology of the self, and Anderson seems to think that at this point my view, while going in the right direction itself, is probably not Kierkegaard's own view.

Well, perhaps Anderson is right. Kierkegaard is a complex and difficult thinker, and certainly there are a number of interpretations of his thought that are plausible. And in fact I suspect that the majority of interpreters of Kierkegaard will agree with Anderson and not with me on the disputed point. But let me try to make a case for my view. (For a fuller development of my views, including my account of Kierkegaard, see Evans [2006].)

The key passage in dispute is one from Kierkegaard's *The Sickness Unto Death* in which Kierkegaard's Christian pseudonym Anti-Climacus says that the self can only "relate itself to itself" by relating itself to "another," and that the self that is not properly related to the "power" that grounds the self finds itself in despair (Kierkegaard, 1980, pp. 13-14). These passages are frequently read, as Anderson does, as referring to God as the "other" or "power" that makes the self a self.

However, I believe there are good reasons for not being too hasty with this identification. Anti-Climacus is a Christian thinker who is not afraid to use theologically specific language. His choice of the abstract language he uses in these passages is thus highly suggestive. And there are two other points that suggest the identification of "the other" with God is hasty. First, Anti-Climacus tells us that although God created the human self, God endows that self with freedom, "releases it from his hand, as it were" (Kierkegaard, 1980, p.16). This means, I think, that although God is the intended ground of the self's true identity, God allows the self to form itself on the basis of other "powers" than himself. The second point is that in part II of *The Sickness Unto Death*, Anti-Climacus tells us that in Part I he has only looked at the self from a human point of view, and that only now, in part II, is he going to look at the self in clear relation to God (Kierkegaard, p.79).

All of this is illuminated by a passage in which Anti-Climacus describes the kinds of relations that can form a self. Every self, he says, requires a "criterion" or "measuring-stick," and this criterion is always provided by some ideal derived from a relation to something outside the self (Kierkegaard, 1980, pp. 79-80; all the rest of what I say in this paragraph is just exegesis of this passage). A cattleman whose identity is found in his superiority to his cows is not truly a self, because "a criterion is lacking." We might say his standard of personhood (that he is superior to a cow) is too low. Anti-Climacus goes on to say that a child becomes a self through getting a criterion from his parents, and truly becomes an adult when society or the state provides a criterion distinct from his parents. Here is a clear statement that Kierkegaard acknowledges that the human self is formed through relations with other human selves, not simply through a relation to God.

Of course, ultimately, Kierkegaard thinks that a human self becomes fully itself only through a relation to God. The problem is not that relations to other humans are not important; it is that they threaten to become all-important. For Kierkegaard, the relation to God is liberating, since if my sense of identity is grounded in God, I am freed from social conformism and free to become the self God is calling me to become.

If there is a problem with Kierkegaard's view of the self, and I believe there is, it lies, not in his ontology, but in his account of the ethical formation of the self. Kierkegaard's own sad experience of the church in his time did not give him any reason to see that God's call to become the self was a call that could come to him through other human relations. He saw the church in Christendom more as part of the problem than as part of the solution. I think he was wrong here, but his error is a challenge to contemporary Christians to make the church the reality that it should be: a vehicle for God's call and God's grace in helping us meet that call, and not simply a way of baptizing human culture.

Let me end with one point on the substance of Anderson's essay. Though I do not think I disagree with what Anderson is trying to say, I am not sure I like his choice of terminology at a key point. He says that he wants to see human persons as having a "spiritual core that is non-religious, though with the potential for religious expression." If the idea here is that the spiritual core of a person can be filled by things that are not obviously religious in character, then I am in full agreement. However, I would want to claim, and I hope Anderson would agree, that this spiritual core is a gift of God and can only be fully realized through a relation to God. If this is right, then I think it is misleading to describe this core as "non-religious" in character. In fact, if we take "religion" in its etymological sense as that which "binds" a person, I would want to affirm the Augustinian view that human persons are intrinsically and inescapably religious, even if their religion takes the form of the worship of mammon.

C. Stephen Evans is University Professor of Philosophy and the Humanities, Baylor University. His email address is C_Stephen_Evans@baylor.edu

References

Evans, C. S. (2006). Who is the other in *The Sickness Unto Death?* God and human relations in the constitution of the self. In C. S. Evans (Ed.), *Kierkegaard on Faith and the Self*, pp. 263-276. Waco, TX: Baylor University Press, 2006.

Kierkegaard, S. (1980). *The sickness unto death* (Trans.and ed. by H. V. Hong & E. H. Hong). Princeton: Princeton University Press, 1980.

Respecting Ourselves as Christian Therapists
Deborah van Deusen Hunsinger
Princeton Theological Seminary

The basic question that Ray Anderson seems to be addressing in this essay is: How can a Christian psychologist function with integrity when working therapeutically with non-Christians?

He wants to affirm the essentially spiritual nature of what it means to be human as the "common ground" on which both Christians and non-Christians can meet. By "spiritual," Anderson means that we are incapable of being (or becoming) human apart from our relationship to others. We are created for relationship with others which is the very "basis for our own spiritual identity." As he says elsewhere, "The divine image is not a religious quality of the individual person, but a spiritual reality expressed through the interchange of persons in relation" (Anderson, 1995, p. 238).

All persons are thus spiritual; religious persons express that spirituality in a particular way, through various rituals, practices, and beliefs. If a Christian therapist works with someone of another (or no) religious background, Anderson wants that therapist to respect the otherness of the other and not impose theological concepts or religious definitions that the other might find alien. At the same time, he is concerned about the conceptual adequacy of so-called "secular" psychology which, he argues, cannot afford to dismiss or ignore our essentially spiritual nature if it is to be a true scientific endeavor. ("The nature of the object to be known determines the method for knowing.") If the object to be known is the human being and if human beings are essentially spiritual, then psychology needs to include spirituality in its mode of inquiry.

In other words, Anderson's "holistic" psychology is an attempt to make the spirituality of persons the central key that identifies their humanity whether or not they are "religious." Both Christian and non-Christian therapists can operate from such a "holistic" theoretical framework because all persons are spiritual. Following Bonhoeffer, Anderson dubs his holistic psychology as "nonreligious." Anderson quotes Bonhoeffer: "The individual personal spirit lives solely by virtue of sociality. Only in interaction with one another is the spirit of human beings ever revealed; this is the essence of spirit, to be oneself through being in the other."

The problem with this as a definition of spirituality, as I see it, is the ambiguity in the word "sociality." If Bonhoeffer (and Anderson) mean that we live solely by virtue of our relationships *with God and* other human beings, then I am in agreement. I don't want the vertical dimension to be collapsed into the horizontal. For if "God is spirit, and those who worship him must worship in spirit and truth" (John 4:24); if we live by virtue of God's Spirit being breathed into our mortal frame, and if we die by virtue of its departure, then our "spirituality" is completely dependent upon the Holy Spirit of God. We are spiritual beings solely by the power of God, and we grow spiritually only by virtue of our relationship to God and others. I agree with Anderson's (and Bonhoeffer's) point that Adam was not fully human apart from his partnership with Eve, but his relationship with God nevertheless remained primary. Even our (horizontal) relationships to others (*koinonia*) are mediated by the Spirit. The Holy Spirit not only binds the Father to the Son, but also Jesus Christ to the church, the church to Jesus Christ, the members of his body to one another, and the church to the world.

I must admit that I find Anderson's terminology confusing. In particular, his use of the phrase "nonreligious Christian psychology" is mystifying to me (as is his earlier term, "secular sacrament"). If a psychology is Christian, how then is it nonreligious? What would it mean for holistic psychology "to communicate, confer and affirm in a nonreligious way what in theology we call grace, forgiveness and even absolution"? If someone has harmed me and I want to forgive him, offering him the grace and forgiveness of God, how can I do all this apart from language whose web of meaning is intrinsically and irreducibly Christian? How might I communicate this in a "nonreligious" way? If I use words to communicate my intent (to offer absolution), then I cannot imagine those words apart from their specifically Christian (and therefore religious) meaning. I can communicate acceptance, unconditional positive regard, solidarity, even genuine love toward this person who has hurt me, but if I want to stand with him before God as a fellow-sinner, not standing in judgment of him but assuring him of God's forgiveness as well as my own, I don't see how I can do this without using specific theological terms, made meaningful through centuries of distinctively Christian use.

One might be able to communicate something *similar* to grace, forgiveness, and absolution, in other words, but the radical loss of the multilayered richness of context-dependent theological meaning in Anderson's proposal concerns me.

None of this seems necessary. Why can't a Christian psychologist be fully and wholeheartedly Christian when meeting with people of other faiths (or no faith)? Why reduce what we have to offer to some common denominator? We can be ourselves in full integrity, respecting the beliefs of others even as we also respect our own. Naturally therapy is no place for proselytizing, but a Christian therapist should be free to draw on his or her own distinctive theological understanding when it would illuminate or deepen the conversation. There are some things that just cannot be "translated" into another idiom. As I understand it, the uniqueness of the gospel is essentially untranslatable. It can only be approximated in other terms. As Barth writes:

> What other word speaks of the covenant between God and man? What other of its character as the work of God, and indeed of the effective and omnipotent grace of God on the basis of eternal love and election? What other of the fulfillment of this covenant in the humiliation of God for the exaltation of man? What other of a comprehensive justification of man by God and sanctification for Him? What other of the fact that this reconciliation of God with man and man with God is no mere idea but a once-for-all event? . . . What other is directed so concretely to each and all men? (Barth, 1961, 107-108).

Much would be lost and little gained were we to give up the distinctiveness of the gospel.

Anderson's exegesis of Jesus' "spiritual but nonreligious" conversation with the Samaritan woman at the well seems to miss the point. The point of the conversation is neither "religious" nor "nonreligious," as I read it, but rather the self-revelation of Jesus as the Messiah to one whom the Jews would have considered a "sinner" (one of dubious character, a woman, and a Samaritan). Moral rectitude is not a requirement for spiritual communion with the Lord. Anderson claims that the "transforming nature of this spiritual encounter at a purely human level led her to confess that he was the Messiah." (p. 27). But how could this spiritual encounter have taken place "at a purely human level" since it took place with One who is uniquely human and divine? "No one can say 'Jesus is Lord' except by the Holy Spirit" (1 Cor. 12:3).

Similarly, to reduce sin simply to a "distortion of human spirituality" seems to miss the very essence of the concept. As I argue in my book, *Pray Without Ceasing: Revitalizing Pastoral Care*:

> We must recognize that sin . . . pertains primarily to God and only then to human relationships. The horizontal axis, so to speak, derives meaning from the vertical axis . . . . Scripture teaches that disorder in our relationships with others is a symptom of estrangement from God. It is our connection to God that is primary and fundamental. When that is distorted, we cannot even relate to ourselves in a wholesome way. (Hunsinger, 2006, 159-160).

Once again I find myself worried about losing the distinctiveness of Christian language about sin. I do, however, share Anderson's concern for understanding sin, not as an individual matter, but primarily as something that occurs between or among persons. None of us is exempt from the corporate, even universal, dimension of human sin. Yet its primary meaning is not social or moral, but theological and spiritual.

I am enriched when Buddhists are Buddhists, Hindus are Hindus, Muslims are Muslims, and Jews are Jews. I have learned about the distinctiveness of my faith by listening to those who follow other paths. Why can't Christian therapists be fully Christian and respect others as fellow human beings made in the image of God, seeking to live out their calling as best they understand it, even as I seek to live out mine?

Perhaps I am misconstruing Anderson's argument. Certainly there is much to ponder here. I have learned a great deal from Ray Anderson over the years and am deeply grateful for his gifts. I look forward to being further instructed by his response.

Deborah van Deusen Hunsinger is Professor of Pastoral Theology at Princeton Theological Seminary.

References

Anderson, R. S. (1995). *Self-Care: A Theology of Personal Empowerment and Spiritual Healing*. Wheaton, Illinois: Victor Books.

Anderson, R. S. (2003). *Spiritual Caregiving as Secular Sacrament: A Practical Theology for Professional Caregivers*. London: Jessica Kingsley.

Barth, K. (1961). *Church dogmatics*, Vol. 4, Part I. Edinburgh: T. & T. Clark.

Hunsinger, D. van D. (2006). *Pray Without Ceasing: Revitalizing Pastoral Care*. Grand Rapids: Eerdmans.

The emerging or co-constructed Self: A key piece of the puzzle
Cynthia Neal Kimball
Wheaton College

Anderson carefully utilizes Kierkegaard, Macmurray, and Bonhoeffer's philosophical views to establish a pre-theoretical model of personhood. As a developmental psychologist, I am particularly interested in responding to his construal of the pre-theoretical aspect, the "way of construing the various elements or spheres of personal being that constitute the person." (19). I am not entirely sure why these elements or spheres of personal being are pre-theoretical. Developmental psychology, particularly the ideas of John Bowlby and Lev Vygotsky, has rich theoretical insights to engage in the effort to understand *how* these spheres become integrated in personhood, or as Anderson writes, the establishment of the "self's own inner cohesion and unity."

John Bowlby

John Bowlby provided a framework for integrating early affective spheres with mental representation when he proposed the notion of internal working model. Research shows that the early emotional dialogue or "dance" that transpires between the infant and caregiver plays an essential role in emotional development. Indeed, many of the attachment researchers view this early communicative pattern or "dance" as a precursor to later interactions (Tronick & Gianino, 1986). Internal security or insecurity results from the accumulation of these affective experiences (responsive vs. nonresponsive or rejecting; sensitive vs. insensitive) with the caregiver in the first year of life: Does the child view the caregivers as a secure base from which to explore and to which he or she can return when stressed or fearful? In addition to providing a sense of self-efficacy, internal locus of control, and curiosity, the quality of the attachment relationship provides the foundation from which all other intimate relationships are experienced (Bowlby, 1982). There is a type of 'psychological birth' in this process, the birth of a sense of self (internal working model), which emerges from this early attachment relationship. The organization of the attachment system involves the cognitive sphere in that the mental representations of the self, the attachment figure, and the outcomes of the communicative attempts are largely cognitive models or schemas that allow the child to:

> rely on these models…when making decisions about which specific attachment behavior(s) to use in a specific situation with a specific person. Representational models are considered to work best when they are relatively accurate reflections of reality, and conscious processing is required to check and revise models in order to keep them up to date (Cassidy & Shaver, 1999, p. 7).

Bowlby believed that these early attachment relationships guide the individual's view of the self and others from cradle to grave (Bowlby, 1969/1982, 1973, 1980). He suggests that while the early pattern of attachment reflects the attachment figures responses to the child, the later attachment patterns become increasingly a property of the child's internal mental representations, a view of the self and others that is imposed on later relationships.

In order to account for the tendency for patterns of attachment increasingly to become a property of the child himself, attachment theory invokes the concept of working models of self and of parents already described. The working models a child builds of his mother and her ways of communicating and behavior towards him, and a comparable model of his father, together with the complementary models of himself in interaction with each, are being built by a child during the first few years of his life and, it is postulated, soon become established as influential cognitive structures (Bowlby, 1980, p. 129).

One can clearly see the social origins of Bowlby's internal working model. As Bretherton and Munholland (1999) note, "…meanings derived from attachment interactions hold tremendous emotional significance for the child's developing working models of self in relation to attachment figures" (p. 96). Once established, working models of attachment are presumed to serve important functions for the individual. Two significant functions are social information processing and emotion regulation which are key in organizing affective/experiential schemas for relational information and guide anticipated consequence for relational experiences. Social processing provides information consistent with existing beliefs about self and relational others. Emotional regulation helps manage and negotiate distress/anxiety. Previous positive relational experiences build internal coping resources which, in turn, strengthen emotional regulation (Mikulincer & Florian, 1998). In essence, the child, guided by the internal working model's organization and the acquisition of affective/cognitive tools, takes over the emotional regulatory function. This is certainly indicated in the more recent work demonstrating that strong and positive emotional experiences which lead to security in attachment (hence a positive and healthy internal working model) has long term effects on children's ability to have coherent and organized emotional dialogues with their mothers (Oppenheim, Koren-Karie, & Sagi-Schwartz, 2007). One might suggest that a rudimentary 'integration' is being co-constructed in these developing internal working models.

Lev Vygotsky
Vygotsky also made claims for the social origins of psychological development which can be found in his "general genetic law of cultural development:"

> ...first it appears on the social plane and then on the psychological plane. First it appears between people as an interpsychological category and then within the child as an intrapsychological category. ...It goes without saying that internalization transforms the process itself and changes its structure and functions. Social relations or relations among people genetically underlie all higher functions and their relationships (Vygotsky, 1981, p. 163).

Fundamentally, Vygotsky proposed mental functioning as "extending beyond the skin" (Wertsch, 2005) Essentially the transformation of basic processes into higher psychological functions occurs within the child's social interactions and through the use of culturally determined tools and symbols. Specifically, Vygotsky suggests that early on the caregiving adult environment mediates and regulates the child's interactions with his or her immediate environment. The caregiver's words, signs, and gestures regulate the child's early initial behavior. Thus higher functions, such as voluntary attention, appear first in the interpersonal, social plane before they appear as part of the child's cognitive/behavioral repertoire in the intrapsychological plane. Second, higher psychological functions can be understood as the internalization of social regulating interactions or, more appropriately, as the internalization of culturally determined adaptations that mediate the child's relation to his or her environment. Therefore, the regulation of a child's behavior is, first, a shared act, an interpersonal phenomenon (see Diaz, Neal, & Amaya-Williams, 1990).

Meaning is first a shared act, not something that occurs within the individual, but something that occurs between people. In contrast to individualistic notions, Vygotsky believed firmly that intrapsychological functioning emerged through the mastery and internalization of social processes. Wertsch and Tulviste (2005), Vygotskian scholars, highlighted the difference in orientation for these functions,

> In contemporary usage terms such as *cognition, memory,* and *attention* are automatically assumed to apply exclusively to the individual. In order to use these terms when speaking of processes carried out on the social plane, some modifier must be attached (*socially shared cognition, socially distributed cognition, collective memory*) (p. 61).

Specifically, Vygotsky suggests that the caregiving adult negotiates and coordinates the child's communion with his or her immediate environment. The shared processes are subsequently internalized by the learner. Hence, individual differences in cognitive processing can be understood and explained by the social milieu in which the child interacts (Neal Kimball, 2001). Vygotsky introduced the operating principle known as the zone of proximal development (1978).

> What children can do with the assistance of others might be in some sense even more indicative of their mental development than what they can do alone. ...The zone of proximal development defines those functions that have not yet matured but are in the process of maturation, functions that will mature tomorrow but are currently in an embryonic state. These functions could be termed the 'buds' or 'flowers' of development rather than the 'fruits' of development (p. 84).

Vygotsky did not believe that internalization was solely a matter of shifting knowledge or skills that were first shared with a more competent teacher. He believed that the very tools of the joint educational process are internalized, transforming old cognitive capacities and producing new ones. The learner internalizes the process and is subsequently transformed by it. The functional objective is not for the learner to become just like the teacher.

> The focus...is not on transferring skills, as such, from those who know more to those who know less but on the collaborative use of mediational means to create, obtain, and communicate meaning (Moll, 1990, p. 13).

The emphasis, then, would be on the collaboration of the apprentice mediated by the mentor with the expressed goal of helping the novice "obtain and express meaning in ways that would enable them to make this knowledge and meaning their own." (Rosa & Montero, 1990, p. 14).

Summary

There is much to be appreciated about Ray Anderson's pre-theoretical model of personhood and his encouragement toward a more holistic framework of construing the self. Nevertheless, I fear that in his attempts to separate the spheres in order to integrate them for greater 'cohesion and unity' he has missed the wealth and rigor of developmental psychology. Suffice it to say that the psychological birth of the child (or the internal working model as described by Bowlby, the intrapsychological plane as described by Vygotsky) is more a co-constructed model, e.g., is dependent upon the Other, but is not the product of the Other. It just may be that the self that emerges very early in life has a cohesive element that becomes more organized and self-regulated, which then relates to the Other (God and persons) in a differentially established manner.

Cynthia Neal Kimball is Associate Professor of Psychology at Wheaton College in Wheaton Illinois. Her email address is Cynthia.Neal.Kimball@wheaton.edu.

References

Bowlby, J. (1973). *Separation: Anxiety and anger.* New York: Basic Books.

Bowlby. J. (1980). *Loss: Sadness and depression.* New York: Basic Books.

Bowlby, J. (1982). *Attachment:* (2nd ed.). New York: Basic Books. (1st ed., 1969).

Bretherton, I. & Munholland, K.A. (1999). Internal working models in attachment relationships: A construct revisited. In J. Cassidy & P.R. Shaver, (Eds.), *Handbook of attachment: Theory, research, and clinical applications* (pp. 89-114). New York: The Gilford Press.

Cassidy, J. (1999). The nature of the child's ties. In J. Cassidy & P.R. Shaver, (Eds.), *Handbook of attachment: Theory, research, and clinical applications* (p. 7). New York: The Gilford Press.

Diaz, R.M., Neal, C. J., & Amaya-Williams, M. (1990). The social origins of self-regulation. In L.C. Moll (Ed.), *Vygotsky and education: Instructional implications and applications of sociohistorical psychology* (pp. 127-154). Cambridge: Cambridge University Press.

Mikulincer, M. & Florian, V. (1998). The relationship between adult attachment styles and emotional and cognitive reactions to stressful events. In Simpson, J.A. & Rholes, W. S. (Eds.), *Attachment theory and close relationships* (pp. 143-165). New York: The Guilford Press.

Moll, L.C. (1990). *Vygotsky and education: Instructional implications and applications of sociohistorical psychology* (p. 13). Cambridge: Cambridge University Press.

Neal Kimball, C. (2001). Family brokenness: A developmental approach. In M. McMinn & T. Phillips (Eds.), *Care for the Soul: Exploring the intersection of psychology & theology* (pp. 346-362). Downers Grove, IL: InterVarsity Press.

Oppenheim, D., Koren-Karie, N. & Sagi-Schwartz, A. (2007). Emotional dialogues between mothers and children at 4.5 and 7.5 years: Relations with children's attachment at 1 year. *Child Development, 78* (1), 38-52.

Rosa, A. & Montero, I. (1990). The historical context of Vygotsky' work: A sociohistorical approach. In L.C. Moll (Ed.), *Vygotsky and education: Instructional implications and applications of sociohistorical psychology* (pp. 59-88). Cambridge: Cambridge University Press

Tronick, E.Z., & Gianino, A.F. (1986). The transmission of maternal disturbance to the infant. *New Directions for Child development,* 34, 5-11.

Vygotsky, L. (1978). *Mind in Society: The development of higher psychological processes.* Cambridge, Mass: Harvard University Press.

Vygotsky, L. (1981). The genesis of higher mental functions. In J.V. Wertsch (ed.), *The concept of activity in Soviet psychology* (pp. 144-188). Armonk, NY: Sharpe.

Wertsch, J.V. & Tulviste P. (2005). L.S. Vygotsky and

contemporary developmental psychology. In Harry Daniels (Ed.), *An introduction to Vygotsky* (pp. 59-80). London: Routledge.

The 'Third' Element in Mutual Encounter as Existence before God is Jesus Christ
Andrew Purves
Pittsburgh Theological Seminary

Ray Anderson has laid cornerstones for the rebuilding of ministry upon a theological foundation that reflects deep appreciation for the classical or vintage heritage of Christian theology. Many of us are deeply in his debt, for he has given us a heritage on which we now can build. His essay, "Holistic Psychology," is an indication that he continues to dig foundations and hew stones.

There are (at least) two statements in Anderson's essay that, on my reading, indicate the heart of the matter, and that stimulate my response. The first arises out of his discussion of Bonhoeffer: "This construct of the person became the basis for understanding how the Holy Spirit (or Christ) can abide in human persons *without creating a religious dimension alongside the human*" (italics added). The second is this: "I construe humans to be created as having both mental and physical existence within which the actual self is *composed* in relation to God and others."

Anderson has offered a construal of being human in which mental and physical existence, on the one hand, and relations to God and others, on the other, constitute what, or better, who, persons are. Relations between persons constitute what persons are. Over and against phenomenalist and dualist views of human being, on the one hand, and a religious view – in which reference to God is an "add on" to the definition of being human, on the other, and in view of the failure to integrate theology and psychology, Anderson offers an integrative perspective wherein an understanding of whole persons emerges.

Let it be acknowledged immediately, but in passing, that the apologetic significance is to be noted. Here indeed a conversation can begin in which the spiritual core of personhood can be asserted as intrinsic to being human, without us apparently having to do theology. The point of argument, of course, will be that via Bonhoeffer, Anderson has slipped in spirit or God by the back door. Why the "third" element in mutual encounter implies existence before God in the world without dependence upon religion is hardly self-evident. But at least a conversation can begin in which a case is made for a spiritual dimension intrinsic to human being.

I am interested in much more than Anderson's proposal having an apologetic utility, however. Frankly, more is at stake than the tribal rivalries between theology and psychology, and the problems of integration. If words like "spiritual" and "spirit" have any anthropological meaning beyond giving a label to a human experience, especially when placed in a non-religious context, one has to ask where that meaning comes from. That is to say, if it is intended that these words contain some manner of reference to God, Anderson's proposal in which case needs to pass not only a test of psychological adequacy – which is not for me to judge, but a theological test as well. Here, then, is my concern: What is this pre-Christian spirituality? How is this anything more than an anonymous spirituality?

As Anderson undoubtedly believes, fullness of human being and experience is given *en Christo*. Jesus Christ is not only himself the true human before God, but also it is in union with Christ that we discover what his human being as God with and for us means for our knowing, doing, and hoping. That is to say, Christians understand their being as persons in Christ, and assert that outside of union with Christ there is diminishment of human fulfillment, to say the least. The study of the human, for the Christian, has an irreducible Christological center – or better, Christ center. Thus my *theological* question now is: Does Anderson's proposal imply that a Christian (i.e., a person in Christ) understanding of being human is in addition to the core spiritual structure of being human, being a later "religious" add on?

Now the point of reflection moves from concern over an anonymous spirit or spirituality to an anonymous or hidden or implicit Christ. The Christian affirmation is that Jesus Christ, in the freedom of his love, and in the power of the Spirit, is the ground of all human being, whether he is acknowledged as such or not. He is not just Lord of Christian anthropology; he is Lord of all. "In him all things hold together (Colossians 1:17)," including human being. In which case, if Bonhoeffer is right in saying that the actual self is composed in relation to God and others, then that which is implicit must be made explicit: the actual self is composed in relation to God and others in and through Jesus Christ.

It is in part the job of Christian ministry to bear witness to the fact that the name of the "third" element in mutual encounter as existence before God is Jesus Christ. This is the implicate of his being and ministry deriving from the attestation that ultimately one cannot exist in the fullness of human being before God and others apart from union with Christ's humanity. Is this to bring religion in the back door? Not so if Jesus Christ has ontic significance for all human beings. Of course, there is no ground outside of Jesus Christ to which one can appeal to make the case – there is no independent foundation by which to validate him. But if he is the ontic ground of human being, as Christian faith attests, then no psychology can be faithful to its subject matter apart from confessing him as Lord of all beings. Apart from Christ, psychology remains a reductionist discipline insofar as it would wish to offer a construct of the whole person. If psychology seeks a lesser task, so be it.

Andrew Purves is Hugh Thomson Kerr Professor of Pastoral Theology at Pittsburgh Theological Seminary. He can be contacted at apurves@pts.edu

---

Holistic Spirituality? Response to Ray Anderson
LeRon Shults
Agder University, Norway

As one of Professor Anderson's former students I had the opportunity to hear about several of the theological influences he mentions in his article as I listened to his systematic theology lectures at Fuller. Over the years I have learned more about the resources that shaped his own development by trying to keep up with his publications. It was wonderful to have the whole narrative outlined in a single presentation. In a sense I feel like this is part of my own story. Ray's life and theology were a huge factor not only in my decision to become a theologian in the first place, but also in my (ongoing) attempt to become a particular kind of theologian—one who does theology for the sake of the transformation of persons in community and who attends to the insights of other disciplines, especially psychology, in this theological task.

It will therefore not be much of a surprise that I agree with most of what Ray has proposed in his article. His basic goal, as I understand it, is to develop a model of the human person that can help counsellors pass through the horns of an apparent dilemma: *either* accept an explicitly religious (Christian) theoretical model and practice *or* adopt an allegedly value-free (non-religious) therapeutic approach. The conceptual key to escaping this dilemma is a model of holistic psychology (and holistic Christian therapeutic practice) that distinguishes between the *spiritual* and the *religious* dimensions of personal life. The spiritual, which is the core of human personhood, is pre-religious—i.e., prior to particular expressions of religious thought or practice. This allows the Christian therapist to facilitate the healing of a person's spirituality without necessarily and immediately addressing concrete or explicit religious beliefs. Ray goes out of his way to depict spirituality in relational terms, building on the work of Barth, Torrance, Macmurray, and Bonhoeffer, among others.

I wholly (!) agree with the goal as well as the relational orientation of the model, but rather than taking up any more space rejoicing over the consensus I still share with my mentor, I will use this opportunity to invite clarification on a few points related to his model. There are three aspects of the formulation that seem to work against, or at least insufficiently support, the *holism* of the model. In other words, I do not quite see how they help foster a holistic understanding of the human person.

The first is the use of the car and driver metaphor, with which the article begins and ends. Ray emphasizes that he is more interested in the person driving than the mechanics of the car. Of course all analogies break down, but this one seems to promote a way of imagining the human person that actually counters the concern for holism. Although I know this is not Ray's intention, it can easily lead us to imagine a "ghost in the machine," in which the soul is the agent within the body. Or the spirit is at the wheel of the psyche? For me, this sounds too much like Cartesian dualism, which I know Ray is careful to avoid in his writings. Perhaps the metaphor is meant only to serve as a negative response to those who too quickly impale themselves on the "(allegedly) neutral auto mechanic" side of the dilemma above. But I would love to hear more about what *positive* work this metaphor does in the service of holism.

A second aspect of the formulation of the

model that seems to work against holism is the frequent use of the term "core." A similar concern could be expressed about the terms "parts" and "pieces," which are also used, but the concept of a *core* reinforces an image of the human person as composed of "inner" and "outer" parts (like the car and driver metaphor). The model is designed to help us understand how "the Holy Spirit (or Christ) can abide in human persons without creating a religious dimension alongside the human." But it is not clear to me how the Spirit relates both to the *core* of the human person and the *whole* human person. Figure 1 places the spiritual sphere under the psychical, and the furthest away from the social, which is where Ray emphasizes the divine Spirit is linked to the human spirit. "The Spirit of God does not constitute something alongside of or merely inside of a person as an individual. Rather, the Spirit of God joins the human spirit at the core of its social reality." However, toward the end of the article, Ray summarizes: "In my way of construing the self, the spiritual aspect as a nonreligious component is fully psychological as the human core of the self." How is the term *psychological* here differentiated from the *psychical* (in Figure 1)? Is the core to which the Spirit is joined primarily the social or the spiritual, or is the core the whole within the brackets (including the sexual, etc.), or is it the social-self which embraces or mediates the cohesion of the whole, or the ongoing integration of the ego-self and the relational-self? I think I know Ray's answer, but I would love to hear more about why the term "core" was chosen to clarify the relational complexity of Figure 1.

Finally, the brief appeal to Genesis also seems problematic in this regard. Ray indicates that his goal is to begin with what the Bible tells us in Genesis 1. But is this really what he does, and if so in what sense? It seems to me that his method (which I like very much) does not "begin" with Scripture or with contemporary empirical data, but within an integrative tension between them. He operates out of his own social (ecclesial) context that mediates to him particular ways of interpreting meaning through biblical narratives, always and already shaped by linguistic and social scientific categories. More importantly, I do not see how the appeal to Genesis really helps in this case. The story of the "Lord God" breathing life into the man formed out of the dust of the ground appears in the second (Yahwist) narrative in Genesis 2, which actually does not differentiate between "mental" and "spiritual" (Ray's terms), nor make use of the concept of the image of God. The latter phrase is utilized only in the Elohist account of Genesis 1. The chronological inconsistencies between these two stories are well-known. The Hebrew Bible was written over hundreds of years, and naturally depicts a variety of ancient anthropological models. I would love to hear more about the rationale for appealing to this text, and whether and to what extent the holistic model must "begin" with or at least find explicit warrant in the cosmogonic myths of Genesis?

I hope that these minor critical questions, which after all are primarily about terminology, will not obscure my enthusiasm and support for Ray's claim that the spiritual dimension of personal existence is wholly natural, socially mediated, and upheld by the gracious presence of the divine Spirit who calls us toward integrating our self-other-God relations in ways that take the form of Christ in the world, whether or not we (or our clients) use explicitly Christian language and practices.

LeRon Shults is Professor of Systematic Theology, Agder University, Institute for Religion, Philosophy and History, 4604 Kristiansand, Norway. His email address is leron.shults@hia.no.

Living in the Space Between Us
John Swinton
University of Aberdeen

Thinking through how to respond to Ray Anderson's most interesting and stimulating paper, I find myself drawn not to challenge or critique, at least not formally. Rather what I would like to do in this short essay is to offer a slightly different perspective on the issues by drawing on another culture and a different tradition which relates to the Western theological approaches that Anderson works with, but in some ways goes beyond them, or at least offers a different frame on some of the issues. I want to explore what insights might be gained from reflection on African *ubuntu* theology and how a wider intercultural perspective might help to deepen and challenge the perspective that Anderson has offered to us.

What is Ubuntu?
The idea of *ubuntu* is an African worldview which centers on the ways in which human beings relate

to one another and to the created order. It is both a philosophy and a theology of community, and a way of life. *Ubuntu* has a very specific understanding of personhood and human development. Human beings are not perceived as discrete, isolated individuals in the way that many Western philosophical positions suggest. Rather, human beings are perceived as constituted as individuals through their relationships and affiliations with other individuals, communities, and ultimately to God. Ackerman (2000) describes *ubuntu* as "a traditional African philosophy and way of life [that] sees all of life, that is all of creation of which we humans are a part, as being sacred." In the worldview created by *ubuntu*:

> Humanity is like a vast interrelated web. As John Mbiti has put it so strikingly from an African world view "I belong, therefore I am." In this boundless human web our humanity is something which comes to us as a gift. It is found, shaped and nurtured in and through the humanity of others. We can only exercise our humanity by being in relationship with others, and there is no growth, happiness or fulfillment for us apart from other human beings. Finally, because of this notion of a universal human web of relationships, no one is a stranger (Ackerman, 2000).

Within this worldview, personhood and identity are not individual possessions; they are gifts bestowed upon one another within community. Personhood is a relational concept that has to do with the individual's inextricable interconnectedness with the relational matrix that is life. Individuality emerges out of wholeness and community and feeds back into the wholeness and community of all of creation:

> The African concept of a person as wholeness does not deny human individuality as an ontological fact, as an analytic finitude, but ascribes ontological primacy to the community through which the human individual comes to know both themselves and the world around them (Ramose, 1999, p. 79).

Whilst this perspective can run the risk of opening people to forms of oppressively conformist collectivism within which the individual is engulfed by the community, *ubuntu* protects and enhances individuality and communalism by incorporating both relationship and distance; accepting others in their otherness without losing them in their distance.

Ubuntu Theology

Desmond Tutu has taken this traditional African concept of *ubuntu* and, by interpreting it within the doctrine of creation, has developed what he describes as the theology of *ubuntu*:

> When we want to give high praise to someone we say *Yu, u nobuntu*'; hey, he or she has *ubuntu*. This means they are generous, hospitable, friendly, caring and compassionate. They share what they have. It also means my humanity is caught up, is inextricably bound up, in theirs. We belong in a bundle of life. We say, "a person is a person through other people." It is not "I think therefore I am." It says rather: "I am human because I belong." I participate, I share. A person with ubuntu is open and available to others, affirming of others, does not feel threatened that others are able and good; for he or she has a proper self-assurance that comes from knowing that he or she belongs in a greater whole and is diminished when others are humiliated or diminished, when others are tortured or oppressed, or treated as if they were less than who they are…what dehumanises you, inexorably dehumanises me (Tutu, 1999, p. 35).

It is this theological perspective that underpins the work of the Truth and Reconciliation Commission and its practical theological stance against torture, discrimination, and injustice and for forgiveness and reconciliation. Acts of forgiveness and reconciliation begin to repair the torn fabric of community and return things to their proper relational shape.

Living in the space between us

Ubuntu offers us an interesting perspective on human identity and development. *Ubuntu* recognizes the individual as "a unique centre of *shared* life" (Schutte, 2001, p. 9, italics added). Rather than the individual self, *ubuntu* offers an understanding of the Self as intersubjective. (This approach sits close to Martin Buber's [1963, pp. 93-97] idea of 'healing through meeting" and resonates with John Macmurray's [1991] emphasis on the significance of persons truly meeting and engaging with persons.)

Within the intersubjective Self, neither the individual nor the community is given ontological primacy. Rather it is the intersubjectivity of what occurs in the space between the "I" and the "Thou" that is the focus; the "I" and the "Thou" come together to form the "I and the 'I'" in the space between the "I and the 'Thou.'" Intersubjective relationships are thus seen to be both formative and dialectical. They are formative insofar as such engagement mutually constructs the personhood and identity of the "other," and also dialectic in that the product of such encounter is greater than the sum of the parts; the developing self that emerges from within the "space between" is dependant on, greater than, and constitutive of both.

The idea of "the individual" takes on quite a different shape within this theology as do concepts of freedom and individuality. If "I am because we are, and since we are, therefore I am" (Mbiti, 1990, p. 108), then to be free is not to be autonomous, but rather to be in right relationship with the other; anything less makes our freedom illusory. Intersubjective connectivity is the goal of the self rather than autonomy. Within this dialectic, health and illness are likewise assumed to be things that occur to whole human beings in their physical, mental, and spiritual dimensions. Indeed it is not possible to understand or deal with one dimension without the other.

Hospitality, healing and wholeness

Ubuntu thus draws out and develops the insights Anderson provides us with in his paper and offers a complementary yet challenging context and frame for his exploration of Kierkegaard, Evans, Macmurray, and Bonhoeffer. When viewed through the lens of *ubuntu*, psychology can be perceived as one of many tools that pastoral carers use to help heal and mend the broken fabric of individual and corporate lives. Within the framework of *ubuntu*, theology and psychology can be seen to be wedded together in relationships of hospitality. In human relationships in order to be hospitable to one another, it is necessary that we first recognize and respect our mutual identities and our potential to become transformative friends. For "me" to be hospitable to "you" I need to know who I am and feel confident in that knowledge. For us to become friends, I need to realize who "we" are. If I pretend to be you or you pretend to be me, one of us will collapse into the other, and there will be no creative space between us. But if I am happy to accept you for who you are and to recognize the importance of the gifts you offer to me and their implications for who I am and whom we will become, then together we can create a hospitable space within which healing dialogue becomes a possibility. This is so for human relationships, but it is also so for the relationship between psychology and theology. *Ubuntu* highlights the significance of hospitable relationships within and between human beings and within and between those tools that we choose to use to participate with God in the healing of our fragmented world.

John Swinton is Professor in Practical Theology and Pastoral Care at the University of Aberdeen, Scotland, United Kingdom, and the director of the University's Centre for Spirituality, Health and Disability. (www.abdn.ac.uk/cshad). He can be contacted at j.swinton@abdn.ac.uk or at the School of Divinity, History, and Philosophy, King's College, University of Aberdeen, Aberdeen, AB24 3UB, Scotland, United Kingdom.

References

Ackermann, D. M. (2000). Lamenting tragedy from the other side. In J. R. Cochrane & B. Klein (Eds.), *Sameness and difference: Problems and Potentials in South African Civil Society, South African Philosophical Studies, I.* The Cultural Heritage and Contemporary Change Series II, Africa, Volume 6. Washington, DC: Council for Research in Values and Philosophy. Retrieved October 6, 2007, from http://www.crvp.org/book/Series02/II-6/chapter_viii.htm

Buber, M. (1963). *Pointing the way.* New York: Harper & Row.

Macmurray, J. (1991). *Persons in relation* London: Faber and Faber International.

Mbiti, J. S. (1990). *African Religions and Philosophy.* Oxford, England: Heinemann London.

Ramose, M. B. 1999. *African philosophy through Ubuntu.* Harare: Mond Books.

Shutte, A. (2001). *Ubuntu: An ethic for a new South Africa.* Pietermaritzburg, South Africa: Cluster Publications.

Tutu, D. (1999). *No Future Without Forgiveness.* New York: Doubleday.

Dialogue on Christian Psychology: Authors Response

An Edifying Evening Seminar

Ray S. Anderson
Fuller Theological Seminary

I read my paper this morning. There was little edification. Now it is evening. It was my idea. I wanted us all to have time to rest a bit, to ponder a while, and to come together after a light supper in this very special place. Edification is a communal event. Laid out in front of me, around the table, are printed copies of your responses, each with your picture attached to the front. As I listened to your response I wanted to see your face, for behind your words is a life, a story, a struggle, some surge of passion caught up in a phrase, severed from its source and risked in-flight between one soul and another. Wine and cheese; indirect but adequate lighting: This is the first time (and the last?) we will be together in this way. Each of us, as Graham (Buxton) has reminded us, brings the piece to someone else's puzzle. Edification is a mutual gift.

My response to each of you is personally addressed to you but intended for all to hear. There is no logical order. I took notes while you were speaking and the dialogue has already been taking place. Here is my reconstruction of it.

Cynthia Neal Kimball

I was a little disconcerted, at first, Cynthia, when you suggested (kindly!) that my version of a pre-theoretical construal of the human self was in fact just another theory, and perhaps not as good as Bowlby's attachment theory. Don (Browning), you suggested that it should better be called a 'pre-empirical' concept, and I will get back to you later about this. Let me give you some background. I have team-taught integration courses with a psychology colleague every year for twenty-five years. I had heard much about personality theory, but little about persons, other than how they act. I soon learned the language, Object Relations is neo-Freudian, humanistic psychology is different from personalist, and each different from existentialist psychology. I knew that Rogerian theory was rather benign and naïve as compared to psychoanalytic theory. At the same time, I realized that in my faculty across the street (literally) theories also abounded. A Wesleyan theory of entire sanctification was not a close friend of a Reformed theory of progressive sanctification. Theories of the atonement proliferated, each with "proof-texts" that presented the aura of biblical authority. Attempts to relate theories of sanctification with theories of mental and emotional health development created fascinating, but rather fruitless (in my opinion), conclusions in our integration seminars. I then remembered C. S. Lewis (1964, p. 197) writing, "Every idea of Him we form, He must in mercy shatter." I do not think that this militates against the forming of theories, but requires that our theories be contingent upon, in the case of both theology and psychology, the ontological reality of persons as created by and constituted by the divine Word.

Cynthia, developmental psychology *does* offer a compelling and cohesive model of the journey of the self, but I keep wondering *who* is this person making the journey: Is the person only a construct of self-expression with an acquired self-identity through social interaction and internal self-projection? Yes, I heard your answer in your paper. You want me to understand that a developmental psychology has a cohesive element precisely because it "becomes more organized and self-regulated, which then relates to the Other (God and persons) in a differentially established manner." I wish that you had put this in your first page rather then merely as a final sentence! We might be closer to agreement than it first appeared. If I were to ask you to tell me how you construe the *nature* of such a person, would you then not agree that a spiritual component is necessary, fundamentally so, for there to be a developmental possibility of relating to God as Spirit? I want to press you at this point because I have a suspicion that "developmentalism" as a theory will still compete with other theories, and even if it wins the day psychologically, theologians will be nervous. Well I make them nervous too! My attempt at presenting what I called a pre-theoretical model of human personhood attempted to provide a kind of "template" against which all psychological and theological theories can be held accountable with respect to their adequacy, allowing for a variety of theories to be used as long as they more or less "fit" the template. What I meant by a pre-theoretical model might be better expressed as a template. I wonder what others think about that?

Deborah van Deusen Hunsinger
I am glad that you are part of this discussion, Deborah. I know that you came close to opting out after reading the first draft of my paper and finding my concept of non-religious spirituality ambiguous and confusing. But we need to hear your probing, thoughtful comments. And I in particular wanted you to push me on the concepts of "intrinsic sociality" and spirituality. From the beginning I worried about attempting to posit spirituality as an "embedded" aspect of personal being without using *sui generis* theological terms to define it. At the same time, I do want to say that spirituality is a theological, though non-religious, aspect of humanity. But you are right in challenging me on the phrase, non-religious Christian psychology. You ask how can a Christian deal with such concepts as sin, grace and forgiveness if these words carry the freight of Christian theology? And rightly, I think, you call attention to the ambiguity of the word "sociality," and say, "I don't want the vertical dimension to be collapsed into the horizontal." Yes, this "collapse" cannot happen, any more than the divine aspect of Jesus' person could collapse into the human. Perhaps the Chalcedon formula that you use in you own writing (Hunsinger, 1995) may be applied here. The "reach" toward God (vertical) and the "reach" toward the other (horizontal) are "unmixed" but "inseparable." I use the term "spiritual" in this two-fold sense.

First, I intentionally use the term "spiritual" in my model to represent what Don Browning has called the phenomenological aspect of the self. I would argue that human persons universally and in every culture express some form of "reach" toward other humans and also toward a transcendent, but often, unspecified reality or power. This "reach" toward other humans I call "sociality," and the "reach" toward a transcendent Other I call "religion." If the same spiritual aspect of the self is involved in both the reach toward the other (social being) and the reach toward a transcendent Other (religion), as I think it is, then a Christian psychology that approaches human persons as spiritual beings in a unique theological way (as sinners, in need of grace and forgiveness), does not need to use religious or even theological concepts to access the spiritual being of a person. The particular competence that a Christian psychologist or therapist has in approaching a client is not that of introducing or imposing a spiritual dimension onto the encounter, but that of recognizing and integrating the spiritual aspect of what might appear at first to be primarily an emotional or mental disturbance. Is this not what you yourself have suggested in speaking of a Christian therapist as having a "bilingual competence," that is, to listen to and engage the expression (pain) of the self as either arising out of an emotional or spiritual aspect (Hunsinger, 1995)?

You ask, "Why cannot a Christian psychologist be wholeheartedly Christian?" The answer is she can! But I'm suggesting that assuming a spiritual aspect of the self, even though it may come to expression in a religious way, such as Jesus did in dialogue with the woman at the well (John 4), one can provide specific content to that spiritual "reach." The "translation," as it were, is already there in incarnation. And in this way, a Christian therapist is already an incognito embodiment of the gospel in such a way that the realities of God are present in the encounter as a social construct before coming to expression as a religious aspect. Of course, as you rightly suggest, the gospel is a theological construct, even as sin, grace, and forgiveness have theological meaning when grounded in the intrinsic spiritual nature of the self. I tend to rely more on Bonhoeffer at this point than Barth. For Bonhoeffer was intentionally paradoxical (Lutheran) wanting to say what something is (Christ existing as community); Barth was intentionally dialectical (Reformed) wanting to say what something is not (knowledge of God is an impossible possibility). A Christian psychology, I argue, does in fact function somewhat like Jesus with the Samaritan woman at the well. The encounter began as a shared human "thirst" for water at the physical level, but Jesus could take that "thirst" and open it to a "reach" for God's promise of healing, hope, and even forgiveness. Your challenge in this regard made me realize that I did not really explain it very well. I am grateful for your helpful and perceptive probing at these crucial points for me to explain.

C. Stephen Evans
You raise two important issues, Steve. The first is in regard to Kierkegaard's view of the self as intrinsically relational and the second with respect to my concept of a non-religious spirituality. Let me take up the first, with some trepidation, as one hardly

dares tilt at your representation of Kierkegaard. But let me have a go at it. I am almost persuaded by your inductive argument from the section on *Sickness Unto Death* where Kierkegaard's pseudonym (Anti-Climacus) says that the self can only relate itself to itself by relating to "another." You challenge the conventional view that by this "other" Kierkegaard has in mind God. The strength of your argument that Kierkegaard here does not mean God by this "other" but rather another human person is found in an appeal to Part II where Anti-Climacus shifts from a human point of view to look at the self in relation to God. In becoming a self, every self needs a criterion or "measuring stick" to provide a relation outside the self. You argue that this is a "clear statement" that Kierkegaard acknowledges that the human self is formed through relation with other human selves, not simply through a relation with God. But then you add, "Of course ultimately Kierkegaard thinks that a human self becomes fully itself only through a relation to God." I am not sure what it means to say that the human self is "formed" through relation with other humans but becomes "fully itself" through relation to God. This seems a little slippery to me. Perhaps I miss the subtlety of the distinction that looms clearly in the philosopher's eye!

Let me tack a bit in a different direction. You appear to find in both Macmurray and Bonhoeffer support for your thesis that Kierkegaard's view of the self is intrinsically relational (social). For Bonhoeffer (1998, p. 54), God, the self, and the other constitute a social construct, with the base of the triangle the concrete social construct of the self. The apex of the triangle is represented by God, but only as a metaphysical postulate. For God to become a reality for the human person, there must be more than an abstract, metaphysical perception of God; the person must encounter God through the same concrete social relation as the self encounters other humans. The incarnation makes it possible for Bonhoeffer to construe God and the other (human) person in a concrete social relation. Thus, one might say, for Bonhoeffer one can be a person "without (a metaphysical) God" but not without the other person. For Kierkegaard, by contrast, one might say that one can be a person (fully) without the other person, but not without God. For Kierkegaard (1984, p. 59), "spirit" is the absolute relation of the self to the absolute (the individual); this "movement" is one of infinite resignation. "This movement I make by myself in my eternal consciousness, in blissful agreement with my love for the Eternal Being." In this way, Kierkegaard avoids the metaphysical God of idealism by positing an incarnational existential realism of encounter with God as Spirit.

The "knight of faith," having made the movement of infinite renunciation of the temporal (which includes other persons), can now make a second movement of faith by which what has been renounced can now be accepted and included. "Had I had faith I would have remained with Regine," Kierkegaard wrote (1958, p. 86). Thus, relationality, by which I mean the social dimension of human personhood, appears to be a formal possibility for Kierkegaard and not an existential and essential necessity, unlike both Macmurray and Bonhoeffer. In fact Kierkegaard goes so far as to say that he has never encountered a person who has made both movements, one of infinite resignation toward all temporal life, and the second, acceptance and experience of temporal life. "I have not found any such person," he writes, "but I can well think him" (1984, p. 49).

You explain Kierkegaard's lack of a social dimension to his concept of the self as an ethical failure on his part due to his experience with the Danish state church of his time rather than some ontological deficiency in his concept of the person. That may be true, but I think that his failure to follow through with his engagement to Regine was not due to the "state of marriage" in his day, but rather to the fact that the "narrow pass" of the individual in his view of the self only survived by a ruthless (he admitted it!) rejection of human love for the sake of divine love. We need to talk about this!

I accept your critique of my view of a "non-religious spiritual core" in the human self. There certainly are problems here that remain to be clarified, as Deborah Hunsinger has already pointed out. Part of the problem concerns what we mean by "religion." The moment we introduce religion into spirituality the discussion becomes parochial. I do agree that this "spiritual core" is a gift of God and can only exist in relation to God. The expression of that spiritual dimension will often, and quite possibly, necessarily take some religious form. My purpose was to provide a "non-parochial" form of a Christian psychology in order to complete what I see as lacking in the more secular forms of psychology and to provide religiously-oriented psychologists a non-religious approach to persons as spiritual beings where the more religious concepts of sin, grace, forgiveness, and hope can find psychological resonance and validity.

Andrew Purves

As I continue to reflect on the issue of human spirituality, I am struck by your comment, Andrew, almost as a throw-away line, that by drawing upon Bonhoeffer I have "slipped in spirit or God by the back door." I had not thought about that, but I think that you are right. You wonder why this "third element" in the basic social encounter of humans implies existence before God without dependence upon religion. Well, as Bonhoeffer said, and I tend to agree, this spiritual dimension of basic human sociality does not "depend" upon religion, but it makes religion possible. In other words, what I have referred to in my conversation with Deborah Hunsinger as a "reach" toward the other person is also at the same time a "reach" toward a transcendent Other. There really is no need of a "back door" through which a Christian psychology can slip in a spiritual (religious) dimension to the encounter. Even if a therapist sometimes has to enter through a "back door" to gain access, she will find the spirit there.

You then ask, "What is this pre-Christian spirituality? How is this anything more than an anonymous spirituality?" Well it *is* anonymous, but it is nothing other than the spirit that the Creator breathed into the human creature. That it is anonymous (present but unnamed) does not make it less spiritual. A Christian psychology assumes the spiritual nature of persons as created in the divine image. In this sense, Christians by virtue of possessing the Holy Spirit are not more spiritual than non-Christians. Dare I suggest that? But it is precisely because of this spiritual nature of humans that we can receive the Spirit of God. Karl Barth (1960, p. 354) said that spirit is not something that the person *is*; rather a person "has spirit." By virtue of being created in the image of God, all humans are endowed with spirit that belongs to God even though embedded in the human as body and soul. I see this as the basis for a pre-Christian spirituality. The Holy Spirit, which unites one to Christ through grace is not an "add-on" as you suggest, but the renewal of the human spirit which, in theological terms, constitutes redemption. Andrew, I think that I can agree with you when you say that, theologically speaking, Jesus Christ is the ontic ground of every human being. This is the form of Christ that can be present without Christian psychology being reductionist, as you fear. Christ is the "image" of the invisible God, the firstborn of all creation, says Paul. "For in him all things in heaven and on earth were created" (Col 1:15-16). A Christian psychology can affirm this on the basis of both creation and incarnation without first of all making Christ "a Christian." I had not thought of that before. But I believe this is what misleads many Christian psychologists. If Christ is presented as a "Christian," then religion (Christianity) has been introduced as the "add-on." Let's think about that some more.

Trey Buchanan

I must admit that you had me hooked at the outset, Trey, by suggesting that I might have a "winning hand," with regard to my model, only to conclude that I might not be playing with a full deck! Your bottom line is that, despite my claim to move toward a more scientific approach to a construal of human personhood, I neglect to connect with ongoing empirical research in psychology. To that I plead guilty. In defense of my approach, however, I offer two counter suggestions. First, I plead guilty to lack of foundation in my pre-theoretical model in empirical scientific data, but not to a broader view of scientific method itself. As I said at the outset of my paper, Thomas Torrance (1965, p. 61), following Karl Barth's concept of theology as science, argued that a scientific approach ought to be based on the assumption that the nature of the object to be known determines the method of knowing. If, as I suggest, human beings are spiritual in nature, an empirical method alone may not either prove or disprove that assertion. This leads me, secondly, to ask you whether or not the growing data gathered by empirical psychology (objectifying behavior) have any relevance to the assumption of human spirituality as an ontological reality (personal being) and further, whether or not empirical psychology can show that such a claim is untrue, relevance and truth being the two issues that you view as at stake in the discussion.

Now, if I grant the relevance of your empirical psychological data with regard to my pre-theoretical model, can you grant the relevance (if not the truth) of my model as at least a working model (such as a physicist might do) in order to expand the reach of empirical psychology to include a Christian psychology that does acknowledge spirituality without demanding that it be grounded in a religious *a priori*?

Don Browning has suggested that I might better term my model "pre-empirical" rather than pre-theoretical. Would you be willing to pour another glass of wine and talk about this?

Don Browning

Having already brought you into the conversation, Don, I want to respond to your helpful suggestion that I am really attempting to set forth a pre-empirical model as a way of moving through a phenomenological perspective deeper into what you call the "sacred" (core) of the human person. I take it that this is also an attempt to construe human being both as a mystery but also as more than merely mysterious, as though "outside" the realm of our knowledge. The apostle Paul seems to refer to this inner core of the self when he asks, "For what human being knows what is truly human except the human spirit that is within? So also," he adds, "no one comprehends what is truly God's except the Spirit of God" (2 Cor 2:11). If he means by Spirit of God some aspect of God's being (ontological) rather than merely a phenomenon, then the same holds true for the human spirit. Thus I would agree, in part, that human spirituality can be located in a pre-empirical construal of the self. However, my model attempts to combine the pre-empirical and the empirical into a holistic model so that a Christian psychology is, in a manner of speaking, amphibious, able to move between the ontological and phenomenological with some degree of competence so that in dealing with the phenomenological aspect of human behavior (ordinarily the domain of psychology) one is not excluding the ontological (usually the domain of theology).

In this way, I resonate with the narrative approach of a Christian psychology that includes the five dimensions you iterate that include *phronesis* as a form of practical moral wisdom rooted in the being of the self in community. I think that this is exactly what Bonhoeffer intended by his construal of persons as social beings whose spirituality is indeed a "sacred" space that will not yield its secrets to mere empirical inquiry but, at the same time, exists empirically in a phenomenological world. Your suggestion that if I took a more "phenomenological tone" strikes a chord—indeed, one that edifies as it also informs.

Marv Erisman

Your suggestion that my concept of spirituality as the core of the social self needs some "unpacking," really struck home with me, Marv. Your comment that our spirituality in most cases is less than pure, indeed, contaminated with beliefs, values, and practices that "confuse," as you put it, our individual narratives, is right on point. My presentation did seem to imply that spirituality is "good" simply because it is spiritual. You also said that non-religious spirituality often dissolves into idiosyncratic, if not destructive, spirituality. This is also a point that Jeff Bjorck makes in his own way. You conclude that we need to deconstruct our spiritual narratives in order to discover the effect of sin on the social construct of the self. Your reference to Niebuhr's concept of sin as misuse of freedom is helpful. I had not thought of freedom as the moral aspect of spirituality. Bonhoeffer's view of the social self does imply this kind of freedom, I think, when he attributes unbelief to disobedience, and obedience with belief. Obedience presupposes freedom to respond to a (moral) claim made upon us by the other, whether the human other or the Divine. In his case, the Divine Other confronts us through the human. A Christian psychology, then, must be able to discern (unpack) in the narrative of the self the nature of the spirituality in the client whether it comes to expression as a religious form or a non-religious form. In either case, what we call sin theologically is already a violation of the moral self as well as the spiritual self. I wonder if this would not meet Deborah Hunsinger's concern that a Christian therapist should be free to "be Christian" in the therapeutic relation with regard to sin, grace, and forgiveness. A stimulating contribution, Marv, and I thank you for it.

Jeffrey P. Bjorck

I can see by your body language, Jeff, that you are getting anxious waiting for me to take up some of your concerns! Our years of team-teaching integration seminars has a narrative and emergent history of its own. We have debated before the concept of a "pre-social" self. Your point that for the infant, "existence is everything that exists," citing Monte, is of course, a pre-empirical assumption, for the social relation with an infant is unilateral rather than bilateral. In other words, the social dimension is sustained entirely from the side of the caretaker at first. Macmurray (1961, pp. 50, 51), however, argues that because love directed toward the child by the mother is intentional (rational), a response on the part of the infant though not intentional is nonetheless rational by its very response. Therefore, while the infant only "feels" but does not "think," the feelings are rational (personal) due to the social construct of the mother/child relation. The fact that an infant responds to personal intentionality (love) indicates that the child is not only human but also social. If by "pre-social" you are only pointing to this intrinsic rather than extrinsic social behavior, perhaps we are not in much disagreement.

I think that a more serious element in your critique is the theological issue of original sin in every infant (and of course, every adult—including scholars of the interactions between psychology and theology!) as manifested in the desire to experience oneself as all-powerful and self-sufficient coupled with the need to control one's environment. In our discussions we usually came closer to agreement at this point when I suggested that rather than the concept of "total depravity" as a description of original sin, "total inability" to fulfill one's own needs was more helpful as it did not convey such an absence of moral worth. I admit, however, that Calvin certainly did not exclude a sense of common goodness in his view of common depravity. You did, however, always insist that there was some "perversity" present in each human soul that resonated more with one holding a Calvinist worldview that includes spiritual death as the inevitable fate of the self apart from God's election by saving grace. At this point, I think that Marv Erisman has echoed something of your concern when he reminded us that spirituality is not as pure and benign as we might think it to be. Rather, there is at the very core of the spiritual self some contamination, confusion and, I would add "perversity," as you would call it. One does not have to be a Calvinist to admit to the need for spiritual renewal. However, a Christian psychology does not need a particular religious slant on human spirituality to make it a holistic psychology. My attempt is to provide a model of the self that is not only intrinsically social but also intrinsically spiritual—a spirituality susceptible to grievous distortion, unable by itself to come to complete health and well-being, and with an impulse to avoid the finality and fate of physical death. If this can be held to be the nature of every human self, then the adequacy of all religious as well as secular forms (theories) of spiritual guidance and therapeutic practice can be evaluated and judged to be adequate or helpful. You suggest that further clarification is needed at the point where I say that the spirit in the self is oriented both toward the other person and toward God with regard to how this orientation is "influenced by salvation," or one might say in a more theological sense, by grace. As Hans Ur von Balthasar (1967, p. 87), writes, "No man reaches the core and ground of his own being, becoming free to himself and to all beings, unless love shines on him." The creation of the original human person was an act of divine love, not merely of supernatural power. Von Balthasar likens this creative act on God's part to that of a mother's love: "God, who inclined toward his new-born creature with infinite personal love, in order to inspire him with it and to awaken the response to it in him, does in the divine supernatural order something similar to a mother. Out of the strength of her own heart she awakens love in her child in true creative activity... The essential thing is, that the child, awakened thus to love, and already endowed by another's power of love, awakens also to himself and to his true freedom, which is in fact the freedom of loving transcendence of his narrow individuality."

I always leave our discussion, Jeff, rethinking and enlarging upon my own views.

Graham Buxton

As our discussion continues, I am impressed with the rich enhancement of my own model through the contributions of others. And I am particularly interested, Graham, in your offering of *perichoresis* as an "event of relationships" that is first of all a human form of the divine image rather than a religious one. While this concept has theological origins, as you point out, a Christian psychology can use such a concept in a non-theological way to depict the open-ended and complex "system" of the self as a social/spiritual "event." I might add to Moltmann's suggestive thought of human existence as a "web of life" with ecological implications, Bonhoeffer's (1997, p. 67) more theological view by recalling his lovely meditation on the relation of "earth to self to the other:" "Without God, without their brothers and sisters, human beings lose the earth. Already in sentimentally shying away from exercising dominion over the earth, however, human beings have forever lost God and their brothers and sisters. God, the brother and sister, and the earth belong together. For those who have once lost the earth, however, for us human beings in the middle, there is no way back to the earth except via God and our brothers and sisters. From the inception, humankind's way to the earth has been possible only as God's way to humankind. Only where God and the brother, the sister, come to them can human beings find their way back to the earth."

Perhaps a Christian psychology can also add an ecological dimension to therapeutic approaches to the recovery of health and well-being of persons as not only involving mental but also physical symbiosis with the creation as well as the Creator. Your comments in this regard provide a threshold for further study and reflection.

LeRon Shults

I was hoping that someone would pick up on the car and driver metaphor, LeRon, so that I could disarm (dismantle) it a bit, so thanks! I think it might have been Karl Barth that once said a good analogy is meant to conceal as much as it is intended to reveal. In my case, I am afraid that the analogy serves to confuse as much or more than to clarify. As originally used, it was meant only to suggest that human behavior (personality) is not yet the essence of the person. I was concerned that one's behavior was being used as the *only* criterion to represent the person herself. And, in fact, the psychologist colleague to whom I referred at the beginning of my paper confirmed this assumption when he admitted that my discussion of "personhood" as an objective reality was quite foreign to him. I think that he really did think that I was referring to a "ghost in the machine!" So we can let that analogy disappear in the mist.

More substantial is your concern over my use of the term "core" with regard to the spiritual aspect of the self. Again, this could be construed in a dualistic way that, of course, is not my intention. I take some comfort in the fact that Don Browning commented that he agrees with me that the "spiritual dimension defines the self to the core." Again there is no intent here to indicate that the spiritual aspect is divided within the self. Rather, if there is a "depth" to the self, as I think there is, then spirituality goes to the very depth of the self. This may be what Paul meant when he said, "For I delight in the law of God in my inmost self" (Rom 7:23, NRSV). In this same context, you raise a good question. Is my use of the term 'psychological' the same or different from my term "psychical?" I confess to a bit of sloppiness at this point in my writing. When I say "fully psychological" I mean to convey something of what I mean by Christian psychology as a holistic construal of the human person. The term "psychical" as used in the diagram is intended in a quite narrower sense, depicting more or less the "affective" elements of the self, which is to say, feelings, emotions, etc.

Finally, with regard to my rather uncritical use of the Genesis narratives as an "anchor" point in the biblical account of creation, you will not be surprised that I view the first two chapters of Genesis as more of a "theological document" embedded in the narrative of the people of Israel, looking backward as it were, from redemption to creation. Thus here too I look for the "pre-theoretical" Word lying behind the documentary critical hypotheses that dominates so much of the biblical exegesis in the academy. I plead guilty, as Barth once did, of setting aside the surface questions regarding textual problems in order to allow the text to grasp me with its revelatory intent. The narrative, read as a whole, does tell us that we are physical creatures (of the dust) into which God breathed his own spirit with the result that we not only bear the divine image but are "living beings" (*nephesh chaiyah*). It might be better to say that I "draw upon" this creation narrative, rather than "begin" here, in order to set forth the fundamental elements of my model as a duality of the physical and non-physical bound together in a holistic unity of personal life with God and other humans. As always, I learn from you LeRon, thanks!

John Swinton

You always bring a new and fresh perspective to the issue under discussion, John, and by informing us of the African concept of *Ubuntu* you have added a new perspective indeed! Personhood and self are not individual but communal: ontological primacy is assigned to the community. We become a person through other people. "I belong, therefore I am." Inter-subjective connectivity is the goal of the self, rather than pseudo-autonomy. Hospitable relationships reflect the "sacred" space that binds humans to one another and to this world. Each of these concepts could be viewed as expanding on the thought of Dietrich Bonhoeffer. If, as I suggest in my model, we are spiritual beings who also happen to be human, the *Ubuntu* could be viewed as an expression of that non-religious spirituality. There are seed thoughts in your brief response that ought to be picked up and developed further as a way of bringing a broader, multi-cultural perspective to Christian psychology. I think that what you have written earlier (Swinton, 2000) about friendship and the role of community in providing a context for the healing and recovery of those with mental health problems incorporates an *Ubuntu* theology into Christian psychology. I look for more!

Summary and Conclusion

I am humbled by the fact that each of you took the time and effort to read and respond to my presentation. But more than that, I am grateful for this event that brought us together in the mutual gift of edification. In sharing our thoughts. we have exposed ourselves, spiritually, to the very core of our selves (yes, LeRon!). Once ventured into the "space" of mutual intentionality of understanding and growth, our thoughts come back to us as still our own, but never quite the same. Edification is neither the result of repetition nor of mere emulation but of a process whose creativity resides in the person, not in the product. As John has just told us, "If I pretend to be you or you pretend to be me, one of us will collapse into the other and there will be no creative space between us." That creative space is where the Spirit hovers; it is a sacred space, as you have reminded us, Don. The dance of *perichoresis* is drawing to a close, Graham, for this particular event. One cannot leave too quickly, for that would reveal the intrusion of other places, other persons, into this moment. Nor can one linger too long, for the dance is over when the music stops, and there are, as Robert Frost (1946) once so eloquently reminded us, other voices calling us to other places. "The woods are lovely, dark, and deep/ But I have promises to keep/ And miles to go before I sleep/ And miles to go before I sleep."

My former teacher, Edward John Carnell (1957, p. 79), concluded his cordial discussion of Søren Kierkegaard by saying that when it came time to part company, he felt something like a way-farer who is joined by another only to come to a fork in the road. "In the end they must go their separate ways, for each tenaciously clings to his own convictions. Though keenly regretting the loss of fellowship, each must courageously venture the hope that wisdom is on his side." And then he added, "We never do anything consciously for the last time without sadness of heart."

Lest I end on too melancholy a note, let us raise a glass and offer cheers to Eric Johnson, Paul Watson, and Tim Sisemore with gratitude for their vision of a Christian psychology, a work in progress which has inspired my contribution to this volume. Hear! Hear!

References

Barth, K (1960). *Church dogmatics* III, 2. Edinburgh: T & T Clark

Bonhoeffer, D. (1997). *Creation and fall: A theological exposition of genesis 1-3*, Dietrich Bonhoeffer Works, Volume 3. Minneapolis: Fortress Press.

Bonhoeffer, D. (1998). *Sanctorum communio: A theological study of the sociology of the church*. Minneapolis: Fortress Press.

Carnell, E. (1957). *Christian commitment: An apologetic*, New York: the Macmillan Company.

Frost, R. (1946). Stopping by the woods on a snowy evening, in *The poems of Robert Frost*. New York: Modern Library.

Hunsinger, D. (1995). *Theology and pastoral counseling: A new interdisciplinary approach*, Grand Rapids, MI: Eerdmans Publishing Company.

Kierkegaard, S. (1958). *The journals of Søren Kierkegaard*. New York: Harper Torchbooks.

Kierkegaard, S. (1974). *Fear and trembling and the sickness unto death*, translated by Walter Lowrie, Princeton: Princeton University Press.

Lewis, C. S. (1964). *Letters to Malcolm: Chiefly on prayer*, NY: Harcourt, Brace, & World,

Macmurray, J. (1961). *Persons in relation*, London: Faber and Faber, Ltd.

Swinton, J. (2000). *Resurrecting the person: Friendship and the care of people with mental health problems*, Nashville: Abingdon.

Torrance, T. (1965). *Theology in reconstruction*, Grand Rapids, MI: Eerdmans.

von Balthasar, H. (1967). *A Theological anthropology*, New York: Sheed and Ward.

Advocate and Judge: The Vicarious Humanity of Christ and the "Ideal" Self

Christian D. Kettler
Friends University

Modern thinking typically restricts knowledge of the human to the empirical. The vicarious humanity of Christ embraces the whole person, but Christ also comes as the priest of creation who is both advocate and judge. As judge, he judges our attempts to create the "ideal" self, for example, in celebrities or in religion. As advocate, he defends genuine hurting humanity by taking their place in dependence upon the Father in the Spirit, revealing not only God but also what it means to be truly human.

The empirical is at the heart of modern knowledge of the human being. But is there a basic problem if we use the empirical to exhaust our understanding of the human? That which is empirical about a human being, apart from brain waves and biochemistry, is the tortured person. What is the true human being: the creature that can be curious, investigating the cosmos with a sense of wonder and love, or a fearful, scared creature, vulnerable to wind, fire, and the grave, often lonely, dejected and rejected, negotiating desperately in a world he did not make? Is the latter the reality and the former a luxury? The empirical is that which Ecclesiastes observes, and leaves him to conclude nothing but "Vanity!" (Ecc 1:2). Nonetheless, even the possibility of Ecclesiastes' investigations speaks of something beyond the mundane (Anderson, 2006, p. 25). Even the most hard-bitten positivist, addressing his "fellow carbon based bipeds" (as described once by the science fiction author Arthur C. Clarke, 1999) can easily let his imagination run wild in science fiction such as *2001: A Space Odyssey*. And why can we write a poem?

The whole person is the object of Jesus Christ, the advocate and the judge of our humanity. No part of our humanity is hidden from the totality of the vicarious *humanity* of Christ. "The life of the self is embodied life," Anderson argues, "with the physical sphere as much a part of the self as the nonphysical (mental) sphere (Anderson, 2003, p. 38). This includes "personal life" and "spiritual life." This is only established and reinforced by the vicarious humanity of Christ, which does not allow any aspect of our humanity to remain untouched (J.B. Torrance, 1981; T.F. Torrance, 1971; T.F. Torrance, 1992, pp. 73-98; Kettler, 2005).

True humanity is not found in "faculties" like soul and body but in the perfect communion with the Father as we see in the free faith and obedience of Jesus. Christ presents the whole of his life to the Father, body and soul, dependent upon his God's will. Therefore, his humanity is contingent upon a reality external to the self. Without denying the deity of Christ, the Son is to be distinguished from the Father, even to the point of a distinct will (see Gethsemane) as Maximus the Confessor (c. 580-662) argues against the Monothelites (Maximus the Confessor, 2003, pp. 173-176). We are as dependent on God's grace in creation as we are in redemption. This we know in the relationship between the Father and the Son in the Spirit: The Son is always dependent upon the Father (Jn 5:19, 30; 14:31; Lk 23:46). This is the essence of his humanity.

A judge is not very welcome in our day. This kind of judge judges our perceptions of capacity as well as deep indwelt convictions about our individualism and our essential aloneness from all others. A capacity to love does not exist in an individual, but only as the Other creates it new by grace. The vicarious response of Christ, the Yes of the Son to the Father becomes our Yes - not just a word but a human movement - a healing act that we are unable to make. The paralyzed man at the pool of Bethzatha does not have anyone to put him into the pool when the water is stirred (Jn 5:7). It is Jesus' word, "Stand up, take up your mat and walk" that makes him well, a word from outside himself, not based on any inner capacity. As Anderson remarks, it is the Word of God that gives us "response-ability." "We are first of all grasped and known, then follows knowledge of ourselves" (Anderson, 1982, p. 56). Our genuine subjectivity is created by the creative Word of God, an orientation to the other.

Jesus Christ is advocate as well as judge, and therefore a peculiar kind of judge. Since he has come into solidarity with all humanity in the descent of the incarnation (Phil 2:5-11), he takes upon himself all the incredible variety of human pain, from "chronic physical pain, the emotional pain of unhealed grief," to "the pain of unfulfilled desires and dreams," speaking with one voice the pain (Anderson, 2003, p. 123). Jesus did this in weeping at the tomb of Lazarus (Jn 11:35). In doing so he was sharing in Mary's prior weeping (Jn 11:33) (Barth, 1958, p. 227). "This is the battle of Jesus for the cause of man as God's creature ordained by God for life, and not for death" (Barth, 1958, p. 228). At this point he is creating a ministry, the ministry of the church, if the church is willing to embrace that cry of pain and cry along with the world. Words are suspect in our postmodern culture, but the cry of pain is real for all. Postmodern culture, however, is to be respected when we realize, with Anderson that "we cannot really listen to pain, we can only share pain" (Anderson, 2003, p. 124). This movement of solidarity is the first movement in the double movement of the incarnation, and therefore, the first movement of ministry. Any other movement is not worthy of the gospel. This is where the world can begin to trust the church. There is no other way.

The Second Movement of the Incarnation: The Vicarious Humanity of Christ

There is a second movement as well, however. Jesus Christ is the one who speaks for the mute creation, who articulates the Father's love for it in the midst of and in spite of the accompanying chaos, including the *hominum confusione*. Jesus Christ makes clear that to be human is to be a "priest of creation," a patristic doctrine adopted by T.F. Torrance (1980, p. 1f.). Christ represents creation's song of both praise (joy) and lament (groaning) to God. He acts for creation, including humanity, doing what creation is unable to do for itself. The vicarious humanity of Christ calls us to the living presence of the person of Jesus in order to seek his mind, to create in us the sensitivity and mind of Christ.

Christ is the advocate for what is truly human. The vicarious humanity of Christ is the basis for a genuine Christian humanism that embraces and encourages human creativity and ingenuity founded on whatever is true, honorable, just, pure, pleasing, and commendable (Phil 4:8). Human beings as priests of creation can glorify God as artists and scientists (or friends or lovers), because we participate in the vicarious humanity of Christ, the one who perfectly represents humanity in trust and obedience to the Father. Is it not incredible that secular culture continues to find value in being human, and therefore, human pursuits? As Barth comments, Narcissus is alive in any age, full of "self-analysis, self-appraisal, and self-description" (Barth, 1962, p. 803). But perhaps our age has an ironic, twisted advantage in that the youngest and oldest of our species tend to be increasingly discarded because we value only that which is productive and successful. Narcissus, however, can never know the true value of humanity: that one stands before God. Jesus Christ stands before God in his faithful humanity as advocate for his brothers and sisters. Noetically and ontologically, we are not able to stand before God, though our countless idolatries, including religion, continually attempt to do so. Only Jesus Christ is able to stand before God. That is a judgment on us, but a judgment that brings good news. Jesus knows himself as addressed by God and he responds always in perfect faithfulness and obedience. While we may think that we want to be addressed by God, our lives show the opposite evidence. Addressed and known by God, Jesus Christ as our priest allows our humanity to be "radically disturbed and interrupted in the work of self-analysis by receiving the Gospel of God" (Barth, 1962, p. 803). (Christian psychologists, take note!)

Christ is also the advocate for humanity in the church. This is particularly important as warning against the psychological unhealthiness of many in pastoral leadership (Christian pastors and theologians, take note!). In the ministry of Jesus, he reveals the deity of God, but not a God who desires to be without humanity. The value of humanity may not be taken for granted, particularly if we are honest about our own misanthropy in any given day of dealing with the irritable, petty, annoying, and trivial among our fellow human beings. A radical disruption is needed to shake us out of bare toleration into the compassion of Jesus. The vicarious humanity of Christ reveals a value in humanity: God takes upon our humanity at every point to heal it and redeem because it is human beings that are valuable to God in themselves, quite apart from their achievements and products (Barth, 1962, p. 799). In a technological, consumer-obsessed age, it is obvious how much of human self-image is gleaned from our reputation, the length of our resume, and the largeness of our bank account. "I produce, therefore I am!" is the new perversion of Descartes' *cogito ergo sum*. But we cannot never produce enough; we can never keep quite ahead of the latest technological gimmick (see Jacques Ellul [1990] on the "gadget" as that which fuels technology, p. 262). How easy does that kind of thinking affect the ministry of the church, when people become the means to an end rather than an end in themselves. God gives value to humanity in becoming our advocate and judge when there is no natural reason to find value in human beings. "Man is irreplaceable, however, because he is the object of the goodness of God, because he is ennobled by it, because God is his Friend and Guarantor and Brother, because God is for him, because God is his God in Jesus Christ" (Barth, 1962, p. 800).

"God is his Friend"! How rare is it to hear those words in the history of the Christian teaching about God. The Society of Friends, the Quakers, are on target when they remember Jesus saying, "I have called you friends" (Jn 15:15). As friend, God takes up our case when no one else really is our friend, or wants to be our friend, when we cry in distress upon the Lord to be saved from our enemies (Ps 18:3, 6). The best lawyer may be our zealous advocate professionally but when the case is closed, we no longer see him. Our lawyer may be obliged to only present our case in the best possible light, but not feeling obliged to admit our shortcomings. (The lawyer is not out for truth but to get us off.) God as friend in Jesus Christ does not simply leave us to our fate but, despite our own bad judgment, speaks for us in the vicarious advocacy of Christ while at the same time not hesitating to judge us. He is the true priest, representing his people, but he is also the priest who becomes the sacrifice. For only in coming under the judgment of God can we truly become free. This consideration of humanity is realistically governed by God's value, and God's value alone, that he gives to human beings. Christ the vicarious priest is the one who listens perfectly to that verdict and accepts it into himself on our behalf and in our place. Since God became human, Bonhoeffer proclaims, we may no longer speak of God without humanity, nor humanity without God (Bonhoeffer, 2005, p. 82). That one thought is more valuable than most seminary courses I ever took.

The Judgment upon the "Ideal" Self

The faith of Jesus intervenes, displaces, and puts to death our vain ideas and the vain ideas of others. What is shattered and destroyed? Nothing less than our supposed exhaustive knowledge of what it means to be human. Theologically and religiously, this is sometimes expressed as the knowledge of an original innocent Adam before the fall. This has a long history in theology, going back to early Judaism. Adam is the model of the intended reality of humanity. Augustine will build a tradition of the original innocence of Adam and leave a lasting legacy to the history of Christian thought: Adam and Eve lived in Paradise in perfect relationship with God.

> He lived in the enjoyment of God, and derived his own goodness from God's goodness. He lived without any want, and had it in his power to live like this forever …There was no trace of decay in the body, or arising from the body, to bring any distress to any of his senses. There was no risk of disease from within or injury from without. Man enjoyed perfect health in the body, entire tranquility in the soul (Augustine, 1984, p. 590).

Human and divine relationships were also in a state of perfection:

> But true joy flowed perpetually from God and towards God. There was a blaze of 'love from a pure heart, a good conscience, and a faith that was no pretence.' Between man and wife there was a faithful partnership based on love and mutual respect (Augustine, 1984, p. 590).

Apart from modern reasons for objecting to the original innocence of Adam (Hick, 1977, p. 203; Pannenberg, 1985, p. 57) is the virtue of what we might call *anthropological agnosticism* brought about by the vicarious humanity of Christ. Even if there were an original, innocent Adam, we have no knowledge of such a human being. The only human beings we know are those who are "ungodly" (Rom 5:6), "sinners" (5:8), and "enemies" of God (5:10). The original innocence of Adam, a knowledge of pristine humanity, becomes *de facto* a non-issue. We do not know who we are in essence. We can send a satellite within a mile of Saturn, yet we remain a mystery to ourselves (Percy, 1983, p. 7). An idea of the original, innocent Adam seems to hide that fact. And why not? What is more terrifying that to look at yourself in the mirror and say: "I don't know who you are!" Psychologically, then, we crave and demand a pristine Adam. But theologically it simply becomes a reflection of our alienation from God. The vicarious humanity of Christ brings this out into the open, as painful as it is.

Is there a kind of Christian superficiality that assumes we exhaustively know what is human (along with God), but never is really grasped by the vicarious humanity of Christ? Our ideas of humanity, bourgeois or radical, remain untouched because of our refusal to admit that Christ has taken our place. Our ideas of the self continue to have destructive power. What is this power? One manifestation may be the power of *the "ideal" self,* a fantasy of our minds, of all that we *should* be (Horney, 1950; Rogers, 1974, p. 24; Smedes, 1983). For with the "ideal" self, we can live without faith. and most of all, we can create our own vision of what it means to be human. We live as if we were immortal. Ultimately, of course, in one sense, we are rudely awakened at some point that this is not so. Ironically, as Kierkegaard (1980, p. 24) points out, our nature as *spirit* creates the despair that one is not able to die.

Human nature can be understood theologically in finding humanity's origin and goal in God, as in Dietrich Bonhoeffer's *Ethics* (2005, p. 49). Jesus certainly saw his origin and goal in God. However, human nature must not be restricted to only knowledge of the origin and the goal. Bonhoeffer criticizes those who restrict God to the boundaries of life, not recognizing that, particularly in a "religionless Christianity," God will be found at the center, in the fullness of everyday life, not just restricted to "boundary events" such as baptism, marriage, and the funeral (Bonhoeffer, 1971, p. 282). Jesus' vicarious nature was a vicarious *humanity,* the totality of his life, not just restricted to his death. Perhaps this is what Ray Anderson aims at when he describes the divine determination of humanity in terms of every area of human life: the personal, the social, the sexual, and the spiritual, and not just at the point of origin or in terms of the phenomenon of sin (Anderson, 2004, p. 89). The vicarious humanity of Christ is a critique of our notion of an ideal self that may acknowledge God gladly in a "religious" way as the origin and the goal, but ignores him in the middle of human existence. Restricted to the origin and the goal, we are lost when it comes to living a daily existence and depending upon our own "variables of self-perception" (Anderson, 2004, p. 90).

Consequences of the "Ideal" Self, Hope in the Faith of Jesus?

In contrast to the vicarious humanity of Christ is our obsession with creating the ideal self. Why is it that the death of a celebrity becomes so significant to us (Anderson, 2001, p. 13)? What is this but the celebrity as the "ideal" self that we would like to be, but which we eventually admit we can never be. The "ideal" self serves a "vicarious" function, but it is a vicariousness that is a fiction. Our celebrities can never live up to the burden we give them. Bob Dylan (2004, p. 121) comments candidly on this in his autobiographical *Chronicles, Volume One.* He paints a grim picture of how it feels never being able to go to lunch without knowing that someone is looking at you, whispering about you, how dehumanizing that is. Celebrities are only human with typical human desires, but we want them to be gods and goddesses. In the documentary film, *No Direction Home* (Scorsese, 2005), Dylan anguishes, telling of his puzzlement at how, in the sixties, he was expected to the "the spokesman of the generation." People were looking to him for "the answer." He had no intention or desire to be any kind of spokesman, let alone messiah, and almost comically tried to distance himself by releasing albums of country western songs and old standards (including "Blue Moon"!). The cult of the tabloid newspaper in subsequent years has only reinforced that obsession. We certainly have always had heroes, but they are transformed by the ideal self into gods. As gods, they will eventually fail.

Communities are not always good. The community may be seen as a manifestation of the ideal self when it is not brought under the judgment of the vicarious humanity of Christ. Human beings are created in co-humanity, dependent upon one another, but dependence is not the same as "co-dependence," a pathological "group-think" that enslaves the individual to a particular ideology or cause (see Hoffer, 1963). The vicarious humanity of Christ provides a basis, however, to be in community, but without the community called upon be its own *telos.* For Christ, having taken the place of humanity, including humanity in community, enables communities - heralded by the church as the representative of the new humanity - to have a center outside of themselves, to transcend themselves, in Langdon Gilkey's words (1979, pp. 210-211). The soul of such a community very naturally bereaves in the loss of one of its members (Anderson, 2001, p. 48). There is nothing ideal about that. In fact, the very opposite of the ideal self is the self that ends in death. But will anyone notice when I die? The community will, and in the vicarious humanity of Christ, that community is not alone in its lament. Christ cries along with and for the sake of the community, as he did in Gethsemane and on Calvary. Christ represents the soul of the community, for it is he who truly prays the psalms of lament, psalms that represent the whole self lamenting: "My soul thirsts for God …" (Ps 42:2) (Anderson, 2001, p. 59). Jesus is thirsting as the community is thirsting. We do not thirst alone. "I have a baptism with which to be baptized, and what stress I am under until it is completed!" Jesus cries (Lk12:49). At the bottom of his soul, Jesus cries (Jn 12:27; Heb 5:7). His entire being, embracing our entire being, cries to the Father (Anderson, 2001, p. 91).

Spirituality, therefore, is not found in a religious niche, but in the whole of life, where Christ has taken upon the whole of our humanity (Anderson, 2001, p. 66). This is a stunning rebuke to the "ideal" self who does not possess this wholeness but a perverted use of fantasy that ends up condemning and betraying. The soul itself cannot be this center, as is found in many expressions of "spirituality," for it is Christ's cry to the Father, embracing the entirety of our humanity as our representative that displaces any attempt by the soul to become the "ideal" self, and thus, a false god (Anderson, 2001, p. 69).

The vicarious humanity of Christ displaces the "ideal" self that seeks to present an ideal humanity devoid of pain: the "spiritual" self. This self also cannot deal with loss (Anderson, 2003, pp. 58-60). Such a view can become devastating for ministry. How can one minister to someone in deep pain or loss without acknowledging the reality of that suffering? What in effect happens is that the first movement of the incarnation, the "humanward" movement, from God to us, is denied, and thus ministry becomes inhuman, something that happens more often than we want to admit. In the humanward movement of God in Jesus Christ, an identification has been made with our feelings. There is much more to salvation than this, but it is not less than this solidarity. This solidarity, in fact, is the crucial first step of God, the only "preparing of the way" for the "Godward" step, the vicarious faith and obedience of Christ. This can also be a critique of spiritualities of "self-emptying"

that, as Anderson astutely observes, empty the self of its humanity (Anderson, 2003, p. 64). Barth's words are wise: If faith in its negative form is indeed an emptying, then it is certainly an emptying of all the results of such practices of self-emptying (Barth, 1956, p. 629).

In a nutshell, the "ideal" self does not know itself for the "ideal" is a fiction. As Kant argues, the human mind is quite active, but the activity of the mind has no necessary relation to things are they are (Kant, 1966). This is also the problem with all sorts of Idealism in philosophy, from Plato to Hegel. We may have a very logical or very aesthetically pleasing worldview, logical within itself, but with one thing missing: it does not exist. In Woody Allen's (1985) comic fantasy film, *The Purple Rose of Cairo,* the despairing housewife played by Mia Farrow seeks refuge in the fantasy of the depression-era movie house. One day, fantastically, the gorgeous leading man played by Jeff Bridges actually leaves the movie reality and enters into the housewife's life. She falls in love with him. Should she go back to his "movie reality" with him? She agonizes: He's got everything: he's kind, loving, good-looking, except for one thing: he does not exist. "Oh, you can't have everything!" she concludes.

The "ideal" self is a picture of how we would like to be, but it has only the semblance of empty aesthetics: it is only a picture, "projected idealistically, positivistically, or existentially, scientifically or mythologically, with or without a moral purpose, pessimistically or lightheartedly, yet always with an unhealthy naivety and one-sidedness" (Barth, 1962, p. 771). Like the world as a whole, the "ideal" self thinks it knows itself, but is simply "groping in the dark," in Barth's words. The legacy of postmodernism is a cacophony of voices proclaiming their integrity to possess their own voices, but eventually all playing off against each other. The call for tolerance by the postmodern is assumed to be the bedrock value. But can divergent views still be maintained? Inevitably there will be the voices of protest that claim the entire enterprise of disparate voices in literature, philosophy, humanities, and the sciences must be harmonized for the sake of peace. Ray Bradbury's famous nightmare of totalitarian censorship in the future, *Fahrenheit 451,* will become the reality (Bradbury, 1953). Books are not only banned but set on fire by "firemen." Why? The veteran fireman exhorts the inquisitive younger man, Montag: You will inevitably become curious what is in these books, the older man exhorts. But do not bother. They are a waste of time, being filled with contradictory ideas that tear people apart. But they must be silenced so that humanity does not waste its life in turmoil. So Montag's wife is busy with the interactive television wall of her soap opera. The ideal self will seek for peace at any price. But what is sacrificed is any real knowledge of the self. To know one's origin and goal may not be sufficient, but even that is missing in the world (Barth, 1962, p. 769). The world has no basis even to make a judgment on itself or anything else, including Jesus Christ.

The "ideal" self is constantly tempted to avoid that "lostness" by embracing a tyrannical ideal. Christ is honest enough to present us with our lostness because he is first of all the one who says, "Your sins are forgiven" (Mk 2:5). But only he can do that; it is a vicarious act. Barth's words are beautiful and to the point: "To know men is to see and understand that, as surely as Jesus Christ died and rose again for all, the grace of God has reference and is promised and addressed to all" (Barth, 1962, p. 771). The "ideal" self is a basic dishonesty with the self and the world: one that does not want to face how one looks in the mirror in the morning: with blurry, dark, and sagging eyes and an unkempt and unclean face. Christ acknowledges that and knows the world as it is. But he also knows that is not the whole story: "For the world as seen in all its distinctions, antitheses, and inner contradictions and yet as seen in relation to Jesus Christ and therefore originally and definitely with God, is the world as it really is" (Barth, 1962, p. 771). What the world is, is to be caught up into the vicarious faith and obedience of Jesus Christ.

Christian D. Kettler is Professor of Theology and Philosophy at Friends University in Wichita, Kansas. He can be reached at kettler@friends.edu.

References

Allen, W. (Director). (1985). *The purple rose of Cairo*. United States: MGM.

Anderson, R.S. (2006), *Exploration into God: Sermonic meditations on the book of Ecclesiastes*. Eugene, OR: Wipf and Stock.

Anderson, R.S. (2001), *The new age of soul: Spiritual wisdom for a new millennium*. Eugene, OR: Wipf and Stock.

Anderson, R.S. (1982), *On being human: Essays in theological anthropology*. Grand Rapids, MI: Eerdmans.

Anderson, R.S. (2003), *Spiritual caregiving as secular sacrament: A practical theology for professional caregivers*. London and N0ew York: Jessica Kingsley Publishers.

Anderson, R.S. (2004), "Theological anthropology." In G. Jones (Ed.), *The Blackwell companion to modern theology* (pp. 82-94). Malden, MA: Blackwell.

Augustine (1984), *The city of God*. London: Penguin Books.

Barth, K. (1968), *Christ and Adam*. New York: Macmillan.

Barth, K. (1956), *Church dogmatics*. IV/1. Edinburgh: T & T Clark.

Barth, K. (1958), *Church dogmatics*, IV/2. Edinburgh: T & T Clark.

Barth, K. (1962), *Church dogmatics*, IV/3.2. Edinburgh: T & T Clark.

Bonhoeffer, D. (2005), *Ethics*. Dietrich Bonhoeffer Works, Volume 6. Minneapolis, MN: Fortress Press.

Bonhoeffer, D. (1971), *Letters and papers from prison*. New Greatly Enlarged Edition. New York: Macmillan.

Bradbury, R. (1953), *Fahrenheit 451*. New York: Ballantine Books.

Clarke, A. C. (1999). *Greetings carbon-based bipeds! Collected essays 1934-1938*. New York: St. Martin's Press.

Dylan, B. (2004), *Chronicles, Volume One*. New York: Simon and Schuster.

Ellul, J. (1990), *The technological bluff*. Grand Rapids, MI: Eerdmans.

Gilkey, Langdon (1979), *Message and existence: An introduction to Christian theology*. Minneapolis, MN: The Seabury Press.

Hick, J. (1977), *Evil and the God of love*. Revised Edition. San Francisco: Harper and Row.

Hoffer, E. (1963), *The true believer: Thoughts on the nature of mass movements*. New York: Times, Inc.

Horney, K. (1950), *Neurosis and mental health*. New York: Norton.

Kant, I. (1966), *Critique of pure reason*. Garden City, NY: Anchor Books.

Kettler, C. D. (2005), *The God who believes: faith, doubt, and the vicarious humanity of Christ*. Eugene, OR: Cascade Books.

Kierkegaard, S. (1980), *The Sickness unto death*. Princeton, NJ: Princeton University Press.

Macmurray, J. (1991), *Persons in relation*. Atlantic Highlands, NJ: Humanities Press.

Maximus the Confessor (2003), "On the two wills of Christ in the agony of Gethsemane." In *On the cosmic mystery of Jesus Christ*. Crestwood, NY: St. Vladimir's Seminary Press.

Pannenberg, W. (1985), *Anthropology in theological perspective*. Philadelphia: Westminster Press.

Percy, W. (1983), *Lost in the cosmos: The last self-help book*. New York: Washington Square.

Rogers, J. (1974), *Confessions of a conservative evangelical*. Philadelphia: Westminster Press.

Scorsese, M. (Director). (2005). *No direction home: Bob Dylan*. United States: PBS.

Smedes, L. (1993), *Shame and grace*. San Francisco: Harper San Francisco.

Torrance, J.B. (1981), "The vicarious humanity of Christ." In T.F. Torrance (Ed.), *The incarnation: ecumenical studies in the Nicene-Constantinopolitan creed*. Edinburgh: The Handsel Press (pp. 127-147).

Torrance, T. F. (1992), *The mediation of Christ*. Revised Edition. Colorado Springs: Helmers and Howard.

Torrance, T.F. (1980), *The ground and grammar of theology*. Charlottesville, VA: University Press of Virginia.

Torrance, T.F. (1971), "The word of God and the response of man." In *God and Rationality*. Oxford: Oxford University Press (pp. 133-164).

The Necessity of a Christocentric Anthropology for Christian Psychology: Reflections on Ray Anderson's Doctrine of Humanity

Mark A. Wells
Montreat College

Christian psychologists often find themselves confronted with the fact that their field of study has adopted a naturalistic or, at times, existential foundation on which to base their science. This article suggests that there is a better, thoroughly Christian, foundation that is, as yet, grossly underutilized by Christian psychologists. If we take the problem of sin seriously, and understand that human personhood is created in the image of God and thus is determined by God, it becomes apparent that the person of Jesus Christ offers clues to our own humanity and the health of the human soul. Borrowing the Aristotelian concept of the telos, this article considers the utility of a Christocentric anthropology for Christian care of the soul.

Ray Anderson offers a thoroughly Christian theological anthropology that may assist psychologists in their care of souls, since his doctrine of humanity corrects several critical errors of existential and naturalistic approaches to humanity. First, Anderson resists reducing his understanding of human personhood to any single field of study. He insists that human persons are a multifaceted complex of creaturely, personal, sexual, and spiritual qualities. Second, Anderson suggests that it is crucial for a theological understanding of humanity to recognize that humanity is under the command of God as determinative of our existence. Finally, the recognition that Jesus Christ is the one true human stirs us to examine the incarnation for clues to our own humanity. Thus, to know the nature of human persons one must think theologically as well as sociologically, psychologically, biologically, and existentially. This essay will work toward a theological foundation for the psychological study of human persons.

Anderson (1982) regards the creaturely nature of human beings as distinct from the image of God. The creaturely aspect of humanity means that we were created, much like other animals, with a physical body and its needs, as determined by God. Our creatureliness gives us solidarity with the rest of creation. In Hebrew scripture both humans and animals are said to have *nephesh*—commonly translated soul. Creatureliness gives humanity its existential character, thus is often the focus of non-theological anthropologies. The danger of a secular and existential focus on human creatureliness as the subject of psychological evaluation is that it ignores the true nature of human persons as social and spiritual beings. The human being is not merely a highly evolved animal. Only in the human person is the image of God found. Deddo (2002) warns of the danger of reducing anthropology to the study of the creaturely aspects of humanity in seeking to discern true human personhood:

> . . . there is another way that humanity faces a reductionism. That is when no distinction is made between its essential humanity and its creaturely aspects. . . . The capacity for reasoning and self-awareness has most often been identified as the distinguishing marks of the human being. While a theological anthropology will certainly distinguish between animals, even the higher ones, and humans, does this comparison really identify the *humanum*, that which truly distinguishes the human creature from all others? Anderson, following the lead of Karl Barth, thinks not (p. 190).

Anderson (1882) concludes "creatureliness does not contain the *telos*, or final purpose of the human. . . . If creatureliness has no immanent teleology which determines the human, we must attribute the *telos* of humanity to some other source than the creaturely condition under which it exists" (p. 24). Human existence is the result of being human, not the cause of our humanity, "therefore, the ontological status of humanity transcends creatureliness" (Anderson, 1982, p. 33). For the Christian, the *telos* of humanity is not determined by our creatureliness, as in existentialism, but rather by the Word of God. Thus, essence precedes existence in a theological anthropology. Existence may assist in understanding the activity of the essence of human persons, but it can never define the human person. Humanity is only defined when the determining nature of the Word of God is taken seriously. The Word of God—Jesus Christ, the active, present, Word of God to human beings—is what determines human being.

Humanity under the Command of God
Humanity is said to be determined by the Word of God in two senses: 1) our existence is determined by the Word of God when God speaks human beings into existence; 2) our *telos* is determined by the Word of God as the command of God—e.g. theological ethics. While both of these ways of viewing humanity under the Word of God are significant, special attention must be given to the second, since the question of a person's *telos* is a key difference between theological and existential approaches to anthropology. Anderson (2001) suggests: "ethical imperatives issue from the command of God by which real humanity is set forth as a created order and an eschatological goal in Christ. . . . To place humanity under some other order as having ultimate authority is idolatry" (p. 135). The goal of humanity is fulfilled only in Jesus Christ, not in psychological self-actualization, nor in creatively determining our own meaning in the face of anxiety—as in many existential or naturalist approaches to human transformation. To understand human purpose existentially, ethically, or psychologically amounts to idolatry, since to do so would be to allow the individual human to be self-determined, thus circumventing God's determination of the human being. In essence, atheistic existential approaches to humanity urge human persons to attempt to play God in seeking to be self-determined persons.

The essence of humanity—its *telos*—is not intrinsic to the human being, as is commonly held by Western thinking following Aristotle. A Christocentric theological anthropology understands that the *telos* of humanity is reflected in Jesus Christ, and it is only in Christ that human persons achieve their true end. Through Jesus Christ human beings become what they could never become on their own.

There is an existential sense to this view, since it involves becoming and transcending one's existence. However, there is a major difference in that humans do not accomplish this transformation on their own. Only through the humanity of Jesus Christ do human beings discover their *telos*. Humanity is placed under the Word of God—Jesus Christ—as determined by God, since after the fall of humanity, the human *telos* is found only in Jesus Christ. Healthy human personhood is reflected only completely in Christ, not as a moral example, rather as the personification of God's design for humanity. To be a healthy human being means to participate in the life of Christ in his human-Godward relations and in his person-to-person relations. Thus, participation in Christ humanizes human beings.

The humanity of Jesus Christ that is shared in all human beings, even those affected by the fall, is set forth in an understanding of Jesus Christ as the "man for God" and the "man for other men" (Barth, 1948/1960). Anderson (2001) incorporates Barth's view into his theological anthropology, "Jesus is the 'man-for-others' in a relationship of ontological and historical solidarity with all human beings" (p. 136). Thus the humanity of human beings under the command of God is found in our relationship both with God and with others, which is only attained in union with Jesus Christ. Hence, "To be human is to recognize the humanity of the other, especially when it is hidden within a broken creaturely existence" (Deddo, 2002, p. 190).

Ontological Implications of the Body/Soul Unity.
Following Platonic thought, human beings are often divided into two or sometimes three separate parts. The traditional approaches to anthropology divide the human into a dichotomy of: spirit and organic matter; invisible and visible; rational and sensuous; inner and outer; inapprehensible and apprehensible; intelligible and empirical; and heavenly and earthly (Barth, 1948/1960, p. 326). Ultimately these divisions of the human being are summed up in the soul/body dichotomy. However, Barth (1948/1960) challenges the traditional approach:

> Rather surprisingly, the first and decisive impression gained when we address our questions to the man Jesus of the New Testament is that the pairs of ideas with which we provisionally designated the problem are

insufficient in His case. The differentiation in the constitution of man, which they suggest, has in His case only provisional and relative and not an ultimate and absolute meaning (p. 327).

Jesus Christ must not be understood in terms of the traditional dichotomy of the human as body/soul, rational/sensuous, intelligible/empirical, etc. The Councils of Constantinople (381 AD) and Chalcedon (451 AD) have dealt with the heresies that this view of Christ spawns. In Jesus Christ, being and act, soul and body, are indivisible, "far from existing as the union of two parts or two 'substances,' He is one whole man, embodied soul and besouled body: the one in the other and never merely beside it . . ." (Barth, 1948/1960, p. 327). Death does not separate body and soul, rather a transformation occurs without altering, or dividing, or subtracting the whole man of Jesus as embodied soul. Being and act are held together in Christ at all times.

Being and act come together in relating to the other, which allows persons to discover the determination of God. The perfect being-in-action of humanity is only found in Jesus Christ. Thus, only in Jesus Christ do we discover our true relationship with God and other human beings. To be under the command of God is to be relational by nature. Barth (1948/1960) identifies the essential being of man with the soul; however, soul is always embodied soul.

Following Barth, Anderson uses Trinitarian theology to explicate the relational nature of the human being. The triune character of God is found in humans as created for union and communion both inwardly—with the self—and outwardly—with God and others. We must be careful not to divide the human person into two separate entities: the soul being the rational and the body being the passionate or passable. Anderson avoids viewing humanity as trichotomic with the body and spirit being joined by the soul or as a dichotomy with the body and soul being divided functionally, essentially, or in a material/immaterial dualism. Instead he suggests, "To be human is to exist as a body/soul unity that has a spiritual openness and orientation toward the source of life itself--the Creator Spirit" (Anderson & Guernsey, 1985, pp. 115-116). In *On Being Human*, Anderson (1982) explains,

> Karl Barth, more than any other contemporary theologian, has captured the remarkable union and differentiation which exists between body and soul when he says that the human person is "bodily soul, as he is also besouled body." Therefore, the person is not simply a soul that has a body, but is "embodied soul." Soul would not be soul if it were not bodily soul. And body would not be body if it were not ensouled body. The soul is not an abstract concept that is located in a concrete place--the body. Rather, the soul is the life of that particular body, which is a person (p. 210).

The soul is a person's openness to God. The soul is expressed through the body and the body is not a body without the soul. Of course, openness and response to God is the essence of humanity, since it involves both body and soul as oriented toward its source. Soul can never respond to another being, except as an embodied soul. What binds the body and soul in its indivisibility is God. Only if God binds body and soul can human creatures keep any hope of transcendence alive in the face of death. Since God binds soul and body, He is able to create a body in which the soul is related to both God and others. This reliance on the sovereignty of God for our existence expresses the fundamental contingency of human existence while asserting the permanence of human existence as determined by God's eternal and unilateral covenant with humanity.

Viewing humanity from a Christological perspective affirms the inseparability of body and soul since Jesus Christ himself is never experienced apart from his body, even after his death. While viewing the human person as a union of body and soul gives hope to humanity and expresses the inward relation of human beings, it does not fully explain the image of God established by God in every human person.

Human Persons as Imago Dei

It is clear in Genesis that humankind is a special creation because it has more than merely a creaturely existence. To be human is to be an image bearer. Anderson (1982) emphasizes the importance of developing a sufficient doctrine of the *imago Dei*:

> It is the foundational concept for understanding the biblical teaching concerning the nature and value of human personhood. In taking up the question of what the *imago Dei* means for human personhood, we address an issue that touches virtually every other tenet of Christian

belief. The essential nature of the human being is determinative for our understanding of the kind of redemption God has wrought upon human beings through the Son, Jesus Christ, who is the true Image of God (Col. 1:15). . . . As Barth once said, "theology has become anthropology since God became man." In this context, the character of the *imago Dei* (as the essential determination of the *humanum* which constitutes human existence as opposed to nonhuman) affects the entire spectrum of God's revelation. It is not too much to say that the core of the theological curriculum itself is contained in the doctrine of the *imago Dei* (p. 70).

Given the importance of the doctrine of the *imago Dei* for the doctrine of humanity, and the possible consequences of a faulty view of the *imago* for the development of subsequent doctrines, a Christian anthropology must carefully consider the doctrine of the *imago Dei* in order to understand human transformation.

We must be careful to understand that the *imago Dei* is not something God gives to humanity in an abstract sense. "The intent of Scripture seems to be that no matter how one understands the correspondence between the *humanum* and the *imago*, the *imago* is a gift or an endowment which takes place in the concrete and particular existence of each person" (Anderson, 1982, p. 71). This means that the *imago* is an embodied presence, once again affirming the significance of the union of body and soul in persons. Only if the *imago Dei* is embodied do both body and soul matter. An imbalance in viewing the presence of the *imago Dei* in the soul alone may lead to a disregard for one's own, or others', bodily existence. An imbalance in the opposite direction—the view that the *imago Dei* resides solely in the body, e.g. rational thought—may lead to a naturalistic understanding of human personhood. The degree to which the *imago Dei* is perceived as embodied in personal being will radically affect one's doctrine of sin, which in turn will affect one's doctrine of salvation and transformation. We must remember the lessons of the First Council of Constantinople and the Council of Chalcedon: the attempt to divide the human person will only lead to heresy. Since Christ is true humanity and Christ cannot be divided, neither can any human person be divided into several disconnected parts.

The image of God sets us apart from the rest of creation. At least two distinctive elements of being human are connected with the image of God in Genesis 1:26, 27. First, the image of God is connected to humankind's role as ruler and caretaker of creation. Humankind's role as caretaker is fleshed out in Genesis 2:15 and following where God places the man in the garden to cultivate it, and later when the man names the animals. The second element of the image of God is found in the human creature's relational nature. This relational aspect of being human is an encounter and relation that leads to unity in differentiation.

First, God's image is reflected in persons as they fulfill their God given responsibility in caring for the rest of creation. However, caring for creation means the establishment of a specific relationship with creation. As human beings encounter the specific creatures, we are told to rule them. The authority given to human beings reflects God's role as ruler and sovereign over the created order. Care-taking requires relationship with creation as both servant and leader. There is an analogy of being in God's relationship to humans and the human relationship with creation. Just as God serves and leads human beings in Jesus Christ, so too human beings serve creation as caretaker, cultivator, and leader of the created world. The emphasis on the correct human relationship with God and creation is clear in the account of creation in Genesis 1 and 2.

Second, in Genesis, the discussion of the image of God is reserved until there are two human beings in relationship. The recognition of the relationship between Adam and both God and the woman is summarized in the idea of the image of God. Thus, in order to develop a doctrine of humanity one must simultaneously, or prior to understanding humanity, develop a doctrine of God. Many Christian psychologists today refuse to allow theology to influence their anthropology. They ignore both the human-creation responsibilities—although it would be consistent with Christian convictions to develop these—and the development of the doctrine of God that is necessary in order to view human beings in the image of God.

Anthropology is inseparably connected with theology. Referring to the Genesis account of the creation of humankind in the image of God, Anderson (1982) points out,

Quite clearly the *imago* is not totally present

in the form of individual humanity but more completely as co-humanity. It is thus quite natural and expected that God himself is also a "we." ... God exists as a being who encounters and relates to himself. Thus, God exists in an I-Self polarity of being. This is prior to and determinative of his existence as an I-Thou relation to the human person. This explains why Adam cannot exist in an I-Thou relation with God without also existing as an I-Self person in polarity of being with another. The *imago* is not first of all I-Thou (relation), but an I-Self (self-in-relation). When the male encounters himself in the female, and when the female encounters herself in the male, each exists as I-Self but also as I-Thou (pp. 73-74).

Human persons discover themselves in the encounter with the other. However, there is an essential being one must discover that exists prior to the encounter with the other. The being in the act of discovery through the encounter with the other is an essential being, not an existential possibility. The command of God has determined human existence prior to our experience of our existence as persons-in-relation. Thus, our essential *telos*—as determined by God—is prior to our encounter (experience) with the other. However, we discover our *telos* only as we experience the other as a person-in-relation. Existence is not prior to essence, rather it is a condition of our essential nature as beings-in-relation. Thus, theological anthropology must never succumb to building upon an existential foundation—e.g. human potential apart from God. Existentialism may aid in understanding some implications of a theological anthropology, but the theological determination of human beings is prior to existential and phenomenological observations about human persons.

The essential form of the image of God is "co-humanity" (Anderson & Guernsey, 1985). Only in response to God and to other human beings do we confirm our humanity. Human freedom to respond to the Word of God is enabled by the image of God in human persons. We must be careful not to suggest that freedom creates the ability to respond, or that in freedom we create the image of God. Rather the image of God in human beings enables them to freely respond to God and others. To place human freedom prior to the image of God is to take an existential approach to anthropology. To recognize the command of God, which determines that humankind is created in the image of God, is to take the Word of God seriously and adopt a Christian theological approach to anthropology.

The tendency in Christian approaches to anthropology is toward viewing the *imago* as a human faculty: reasoning, moral sense, spiritual nature, etc. However, Christians must acknowledge a communal sense of the *imago* that is holistic yet involves implications for concrete relational existence as co-humanity. Human beings need to be in relationship with other human beings in order to find their humanity. We must be careful not to view the relational aspect of humanity as a function—the function of relating. When relating becomes a function of humanity, the determination of humanity as "good" is no longer a theological determination but is turned into an ethical determination. The ethical determination of humanity as "good" constitutes a post-Fall determination that ignores the theological basis—the command of God—needed for a truly theological anthropology.

Discovering humanity in the encounter with God and others brings us to the recognition of our selves in terms of human polarity of being. Human beings find their completion within union in differentiation. Only as theology understands God in a Trinitarian sense, as a union of differentiation, does it make sense of the *imago* in the doctrine of humanity.

The Problem of Sin

The image of God came to human beings in the Word of God. In hearing the Word of God, human beings were free. However, human freedom is a freedom in dependence on the Word of God. Attempting to actualize freedom independently of God, as the existentialists advocate, only leads to sin. Human freedom is not gained through the fall; it is diminished by the fall. Sin is our refusal to respond appropriately—in freedom—to God.

Sin creates a veil that covers the image of God within human beings. It does not destroy the image of God, nor cause people to lose their souls. Those are impossibilities since they would negate that which God has determined to exist. Rather, sin masks the soul, infects it, and causes it to resort to itself instead of God for its determination. Thus, self-determination is the epitome of human sinfulness. The temptation of the serpent was that the woman's eyes would be opened and that she would be "like God, knowing good and evil" (Genesis 3:5). With such knowledge she could determine for herself what she should do. Autonomy breeds neglect of God's determining Word. In a similar fashion, sin alienates people by creating a false sense of self-sufficiency. Self-sufficiency has sometimes been termed inner-strength. Many proponents of human potentiality and inner-strength advocates unwittingly establish an ethic of strength by seeking to find transformation—as self-determination—apart from the Word of God.

The misunderstanding of freedom follows the first sin. Human beings now understand freedom as "freedom *from* that which binds the self" rather than "freedom *for* that which determines the self" (Anderson, 1982, p. 79). The further human persons journey from the source of their being, the more warped the human perspective of freedom becomes. Until human beings regain a true sense of freedom as God intended it—as freedom in dependence upon God—human transformation has little chance of taking place. A restoration of a theological view of freedom is not the complete answer to the problem of the transformation or restoration of humanity, but it plays a crucial role in human transformation.

Sin is only overcome by the grace of God found in the restoration of our humanity in Jesus Christ—the Word of God. Psychologically, this is a matter of surrender to God's determination of human personhood revealed in Jesus Christ.

Jesus Christ: The One True Human

How can human beings, with soul veiled, infected by sin, unaware of what it means to be human, and claiming self-determination gain a correct view of true humanity? On a purely human level, knowledge of the nature of human being is impossible. The best human attempts at self-understanding offered by the greatest human minds fail to give us a comprehensive and accurate view of human nature and existence. Only the Creator of humanity can reveal human nature, purpose, and possibility. God has chosen to reveal human being in the historical person of Jesus Christ, as Karl Barth (1953/1960) proclaims: "We cannot speak of the being of man except from the standpoint of the Christian and in the light of the particular being of man in Jesus Christ" (p. 92). Only in assuming human existence does God reveal not only Himself to humanity, but reveals true humanity to human beings in a concrete historical form. A Christian theological anthropology does not treat humanity in abstraction; rather it understands humanity within the real existent person. Jesus Christ is not the ideal; he is the concrete form of humanity.

Christ's humanity addresses our humanity in such a way that in the concrete, historical, person of Jesus Christ we are confronted with true humanity in such a way that our own understanding of humanity is shattered.

> Christian theology views the Incarnation of God in the man Jesus Christ as the form of the human to which all humanity must be conformed. But the Incarnation is not an ideal form that Jesus "typified" by his actions, nor a means to an end by which God could communicate his message of love and grace. Rather, the Incarnation was a creaturely and human life lived under the determination of the divine Word, fully manifesting the divine Spirit (Anderson & Guernsey, 1985, p. 117).

The life of Jesus Christ confronts us with the proper response to God and co-humanity as union in differentiation. In Christ, form and content, body and soul, act and being, are brought together and synthesized in the perfect response to the Creator.

The revelation of God in Jesus Christ shows human beings who God is and who we are simultaneously. The I-self relation meets the I-Thou relation in Jesus Christ in such a way that the polarity of being with the other is personified. God meets the human and the human meets God in Jesus Christ alone. Only in Christ does our humanity meet God. The meaning of our humanity restored in Christ is exemplified in the restoration of the human-God relation found only in Jesus Christ. Only Christ can mediate our humanity since only Christ connects the human to the divine. In a very real and necessary sense Christ's humanity is a vicarious humanity.

Karl Barth (1948/1960) accurately portrays the concept of the vicarious humanity of Christ in speaking of Him as the "man for other men." Jesus is "the man for others" in two distinct senses: there is an ontological sense of his being for others; there is an existential sense of his being for others.

First, Jesus is the man for others ontologically, in that he is sent in our place. Jesus Christ is human in our place in order to bring about the restoration of our humanity. "The incarnation did not 'Christianize' humanity, it 'humanized' humanity. Humanity in its concrete and historical form as creaturely existence is brought back into its contingent relation to God and to the other as the concrete neighbor" (Anderson, 2001, p. 139). Jesus in our place transforms our humanity. Jesus Christ does not make us something completely different than we are; instead he heals our humanity, causes us to fulfill our humanity and grow into it. The paradigm for transformation in Jesus Christ is the resurrection. In the resurrected Christ, "all things are new," (1 Corinthians 5:17), yet nothing of the essential self is altered or subtracted. The veil is removed and true humanity is able to fully operate. Since our essential nature is not annihilated we often bring the baggage of sinful habits with us into our new life in Christ. The fact that sin, despair, and sickness are still present even after Christ's work in us has begun means that we need community in order to continue God's work of transformation.

Co-humanity, found in the body of Christ, humanizes our humanity through mutual accountability. The church is designed to be a community of character and accountability. Since our co-humanity is most clearly experienced in the community of the church as it relates us both to God and others, the church is truly the continuing presence of Christ on earth. The Holy Spirit is the guarantee that God will work through His community to continue to humanize humanity. The presence of Christ in the Christian means that we need the fellowship of believers in order to experience and be confronted by Christ in our concrete, historical, existence.

The second meaning of Jesus as "the man for other men"—the existential sense—is discovered as Jesus Christ exemplifies what human beings are in his relationship with other people as always acting on their behalf. The image of God in humanity is activated, unveiled, and found in the co-humanity of Jesus Christ. Human persons need other persons in order to discover the polarity of being in communion with the other. Only as the other is encountered and differentiation is established do human beings recognize their own being as a self. Self in relation to the other is the recognition of our essential self as determined by God, since the command of God creates us in His image as relational. Only in Jesus Christ is the relationship with God and human fully actualized, unveiled, and revealed.

In the humanity of God the Son, the true correspondence is established between human being as "image bearer" and divine being as that which constitutes the objective content of the "image." Now we can understand Adam, Barth would claim; now we can see why Adam as the solitary male could never bear the divine image and likeness. There is no "correspondence" between Adam as solitary male and the divine being, because the image must also be experienced through differentiation of being (Anderson, 1982, 77).

The image of God is not mentioned, nor does it seem to be complete, until there are two human beings—a union in differentiation.

Jesus is the man for other men who reveals our purpose to be for other men. He is man for other men in our place, vicariously establishing humanity as co-humanity. He humanizes humanity through recognizing and restoring the full human dignity of those who have lost their dignity. The poor and oppressed seem to have a special place in Jesus' ministry. Theologically, it is no insignificant fact that Jesus ministers to those who need to hear a word of restoration of their dignity. Jesus' harshest words are for those who ignore and fail to recognize human dignity. Following this logic Deddo (2002) suggests that "to be human is to recognize the humanity of the other, especially when it is hidden within a broken creaturely existence" (p. 190). Deddo sums up the Christian response to Christ's being for others,

> Our own being and becoming human will be manifest only as we recognize their humanity and love them in a way that affirms and upholds their humanity, that is, pursues God's intention for them to share in Christ's own union and communion. Humanity alive to God desires to see others included in the blessing of the living God who brings life out of death no matter how distorted or undeveloped a condition we find them in. This recognition of humanity is intrinsic to Christian faith (p. 190).

Conclusion

Human persons are determined by the Word of God to be a body/soul unity in differentiation from others. The nature of humanity is found in the image of God, which indicates a relational essence within human persons—in concrete, historical, individual, persons.

Sin infects the soul without irreparably damaging it. Since soul and body are inseparably connected, sin drastically affects our bodily existence and vice versa. The relational essence of humanity is also dramatically affected by sin, since human freedom to respond to the determination of God is distorted.

Because human beings are infected by sin, the determination of human beings by the Word of God in Jesus Christ is essential in order to restore human personhood. Jesus Christ humanizes humanity by restoring human-Godward relations as well as restoring co-humanity--right relations between persons. The church, as the continued presence of Christ in the world and under the guidance of the Holy Spirit, is necessary in order to continue the work of humanization begun through the person and work of Christ. The work of Christ alone does not show us true humanity, thus we cannot point to Jesus as merely a moral example or model human being. Participation in the humanity of Christ is necessary as person and work is united—reflecting the body/soul unity in human beings. This is the meaning of the vicarious humanity of Christ, since to be truly human is to be found in Christ with our human personhood determined by God. Any account of human existence and transformation that is utilized by the church and yet ignores the Christological basis of our true humanity, is seriously at fault. Thus, our theology should affect our psychology, and our psychology should most certainly affect our theology. However, when dealing with issues of psychology, the church must recognize human personhood as a complex of sociological/cultural, psychological, personal/relational, physical/biological, and spiritual/theological relations. Only as the church recognizes all of these aspects of humanity can psychological issues be treated holistically.

Mark A. Wells is Associate Professor of Philosophy and Ethics at Montreat College in Montreat, North Carolina. Dr. Wells served as Associate Professor of Religion and Philosophy, Assistant Director of Servant Leadership, and Chair of the Honors Program Committee at Sterling College in his six years prior to teaching at Montreat College. He can be reached at: mwells@montreat.edu.

References

Anderson, R. S. (1982). *On Being Human: Essays in Theological Anthropology*. Pasadena, CA: Fuller Seminary Press.

Anderson, R. S., & Guernsey, D. (1985). *On Being Family: A Social Theology of the Family*. Pasadena, CA: Fuller Seminary Press.

Anderson, R. S. (2001). *The Shape of Practical Theology*. Downers Grove, IN: InterVarsity Press.

Barth, K. (1960). *Church Dogmatics, III.2: The Doctrine of Creation* (H. Knight, G. W. Bromiley, J. K. S. Reid, R. H. Fuller, Trans.). Edinburgh: T & T Clark. (Original work published 1948)

Barth, K. (1960). *Church Dogmatics, IV.1: The Doctrine of Reconciliation* (G. W. Bromiley, Trans.). Edinburgh: T & T Clark. (Original work published 1953)

Deddo, G. (2002). Resisting reductionisms: Why we need theological anthropology. In T. Speidell (Ed.), *On Being Christian . . . and Human* (pp.168-193). Eugene, OR: Wipf and Stock Publishers.

Interview with Ray Anderson: Toward a Christian Theoanthropology

Ray S. Anderson
Fuller Theological Seminary

Todd H. Speidell
Edification (Guest Editor)

*The following interview with Ray Anderson (hereafter **RA**) reflects his personal background: farmer, pastor, and theologian—not "career changes" as much as different phases in his life and ministry, not merely to land, country, parishioners, students—and administrators and publishers!—but primarily to the God of Jesus Christ, who sunk his own humanity deep into our place and time and very humanity to affirm and redeem his creation and children. As Don Browning (one of the contributors to this volume), commented, the editors of this journal have provided a "fitting tribute" to one of the creative pastoral theologians of our day. His 25 published books (#25 being reviewed at the end of this volume) merely (!) reflect his imaginative mind and loving heart offered unto God on behalf of God's creation and people. Insofar as I (hereafter **TS**) have learned to think theologically, it is due to one who thought and spoke in an angular way: in my systematic theology courses, at my ordination and wedding, and in my personal life whenever I needed to talk with him. At Fuller Seminary, most students knew that one could walk into Ray's office and feel assured that he would put aside "work" to talk, and the following interview indicates the kind of pastoral and theological counsel of the enigmatic man Ray Anderson.*

TS: Ray, please describe how a Scandinavian son of farmers from South Dakota became attracted to your key theological influences, from Kierkegaard and Dostoevsky to Barth, Bonhoeffer, Torrance, Polanyi, and Macmurray.

RA: I could attribute my fascination with Kierkegaard to my Danish mother, but that would be a leap of faith! If there was any genetic pool that contributed to my maverick tendencies, it probably was from Norway. When I visited there a few years ago, one of my relatives gave me a family genealogical chart, which had my name on it with my lineage traced back to 860 A.D. There ought to be a few Vikings in that lot who were more than nomadic invaders and plunderers! Speaking of being a maverick, coming from a farm and cattle country, a maverick is a calf whose mother has died leaving it to find its nourishment where it can steal it from other cows. As a result, the maverick is usually more vigorous than the others, but inherently promiscuous. If you look at the list of influences you mentioned, they were all mavericks of one kind or another. When my seminary professor Ed Carnell introduced me to Kierkegaard, and after reading through most of his writings, I took a look at the books on my shelf and decided that 90 percent of them were not worth reading. He affected me that profoundly at the existential level. As the founding pastor of the Evangelical Free Church located in Covina, California (1959-1970), I immersed myself in reading Dietrich Bonhoeffer, Søren Kierkegaard, novels by Fyodor Dostoyevsky, James Agee (*A Death in the Family*), Thomas Wolfe (*You Can't Go Home Again*), and the plays of Arthur Miller (*Death of a Salesman*). I was searching for a human point of contact for the Gospel, something that I had not really discovered in seminary. When in Scotland doing my doctoral study, I came across the work of G. J. Hamann, the German contemporary of Kant who turned down an academic position to work in the postal office where he produced a kind of "underground" philosophy and theology. "In a world of fugitives," he wrote, "someone moving in the opposite direction will appear to be running away." After reading Barth and Bonhoeffer, and after studying under Torrance, I began to "color outside the lines" when doing theology. Does that give you a clue?

TS: An enigmatic but intriguing one, oh son of a Dane! You stepped outside of the lines a few times: son of farmers to the Air Force and agricultural studies, seminary student to a church planter, and then from Scotland to Santa Barbara to become a theologian who never left behind the farm and the church, God's creation, and God's people. It doesn't seem that being an ivory-tower academic was in your genes, upbringing, or temperament, I would say.

RA: It was not that I was an iconoclast, after all: I occupied an office on the first floor of that tower! I will always be grateful for my eleven years of pastoral ministry prior to doing my doctoral work. While parish ministry put me behind others who went directly from seminary into graduate school, it saved me from becoming merely an efficient theological technician. It was in my pastoral ministry that my "ear was tuned" to the inner voice of hurting people and my vision focused on the face behind the mask of religion that ordinary people wore to church in order not to frighten the saints with their barely adequate humanity. My congregation of 250 included eight psychologists who sought refuge from churches where psychology was viewed as not only less than spiritual, but also incompatible with what passed as simple biblical counseling. I did not understand at first why they felt at home with us. Then one told me that it was not because I was indulging in "promiscuous" psychological preaching, but I felt God's heart for authentic humanity in my pastoral preaching and counseling upheld by God's scandalous grace. One of the chapters in my Ph.D. dissertation was on "Living in the World: The Incarnational Christian" (Anderson, 1975). When I began to teach and preach the Gospel of the Incarnate one, my theology and background naturally flowed into my emphasis on theological anthropology. To this day, this is the "river that runs through it."

TS: If I may press you a bit, do you feel more like an individual maverick or a pastoral theologian? How do you deal, both personally and theoretically, with the tension between the individual and the community, the perennial issue of the one and the many? For yourself, are you more of a maverick theologian who found his own path—even though you crossed the lines to become a pastor of church and academic communities—who might after all be closest to Kierkegaard, in temperament if not in theory? For others, how does speaking of humanity as "co-humanity" and "persons in relation" help those who feel alone?

RA: I am more of a pastor who also happens to be a theologian. I began preaching before going to seminary; I preached at every opportunity during seminary and for eleven years following, twice every Sunday, morning and evening. For twenty-eight of the past 30 years that I have been teaching at seminary, I have preached virtually every Sunday to the same congregation. My mantra has been, if you can't preach it you ought not teach it. I still resonate with Kierkegaard's fierce passion for existence in the moment. That is why I preach and teach. At the same time, I fault him for his own admitted conception of the pathological self as the real self, with no pre-fallen concept of the whole person. Following Barth and Bonhoeffer, I view original humanity as depicted in the creation story as psychologically, spiritually, and physically whole as male and female created in the divine image. With Barth, I agree that original humanity before the fall occurs within history even though this event cannot be described "historically" as other events can. But the history of the human self includes by divine determination and definition humanity not in its fragmentary, existential individuality, but humanity as it is intended to be and as it essentially is, a unity within which each is differentiated individually. Or, as Barth puts it, humanity is essentially co-humanity (*Mitmenschlichkeit*). Thus, contrary to Kierkegaard but with equal passion, I affirm the recovery of the original wholeness of humanity as the intention of divine grace mediated to us, not through the self's existing in the eternal moment, but meditated for us and to us in the vicarious humanity of Christ as the place where our belonging provides for our believing, as Polanyi says. But what was the question again?

TS: You covered most of it, but how do you think Christian communities can help people who are or feel alone?

RA: Macmurray made a distinction between an "association" and a "community" that helped me. An association, on the one hand, is simply an aggregate of individuals who may share a common task, but not a common life. A community of persons, on the other hand, shares a common life where each one can be "singular" as an individual member, but not a "solitary" person amidst a group. Too often, I fear, Christian communities become merely associations with no real interpersonal sharing of life. Bonhoeffer also pointed me toward something similar with his concept of "structural openness" and "structural closedness." When each person in the community is open to others, that is, vulnerable and transparent as to shared experience of life in Christ, then each person experiences his or her uniqueness as a gift of life in community. Being and feeling alone decreases one's individuality. Being a functioning member of a community increases a sense of personal value, worth, and identity. How a community embraces and includes those who feel isolated and alone is more a matter of how the community itself lives and thrives than on how it "reaches out" through special programs and activities. Scott Peck (1987), writing on the stages of community, says that the first stage is pseudo-community, where everyone acts so pleasantly and agreeably that all assume that they have reached community. When that falls apart, chaos enters, followed by feelings of emptiness, and only when the pain becomes unbearable does each reach out to the other and real community emerges. Too often we do everything we can to avoid the pain—churches can be real good at that!—and so seldom reach real community. Now I'm beginning to preach!

TS: Karl Barth was a preacher too, not only for his parishioners in Safenwil, but also to prisoners in Basel. Barth revolutionized modern theology with his bold and dynamic theology of God's self-revelation. Your mentors, Tom and James Torrance, continued and applied their mentor's, Karl Barth's, theology by adapting his paradigm (Gk.: *paradigma* or pointer) of doing theology. Tom discovered and reconstructed epistemological foundations for a dynamic, unitary, and integrative dialogue between natural and theological science, and James developed a pastorally-oriented theology of worship. What do you view as your contribution to this tradition that combines the best of traditional evangelical theology with a creative concern to point to the interrelationship of our gracious God to his creation and people?

RA: Tom Torrance helped me to understand "paradigm" from a scientific rather than a philosophical perspective. From this, I developed my own working definition: a paradigm is a theoretical model of the inner structure of reality that would otherwise be inaccessible to us. In other words, following the thought of Torrance, the nature of the object to be known must compel us to know it (think it) in terms of what it actually is. Thus, in theology, as in physics, the reality of that which we seek to know must exist independently of and prior to our thinking of it. Having said that, if one follows Barth, who said that the being of God is revealed in his act, then the work of God (act) interprets the word of God. What God *does*, reveals to us who God *is*. What God becomes in becoming human not only reveals to us the inner being of God himself, but also, and just as importantly for us as his children, the deeper meaning of what it means to be human. Thus, the incarnation is an ontological reality that forces upon us a demand to know God in terms of his "being for us" and to know ourselves in terms of our "being for God."

The gospel narrative is itself a paradigm that demands theological reflection. But in this case, as is true of all theology, theology is the servant and not the master of the event. In my own case, I view the theological construct of the triune nature of God as a dynamic paradigm with hermeneutical significance. In an earlier article (Anderson, 1986), I argued that the risen and contemporary Christ continues through the Holy Spirit to act so as to make effective the Word of Christ. I have subsequently developed this as a form of what I call "Christopraxis" as a foundation for a practical theology of ministry on the part of both pastors and psychologists (Anderson, 2001, 2003). In this way, a Christian theology and a Christian psychology can operate with the same paradigm. I hope that this will be a contribution.

TS: Would you support a new paradigm that is more concrete and dynamic than the early abstract and static discussion of "the integration of psychology and theology"? (Which psychology? Which theology?) Tom Torrance has offered a widespread critique both of theology and of psychology—whether Christian or secular!—as hopelessly dualistic. What would you say to advocates of "integration"? What is the way forward for a Christian psychology that respects the creaturely contingencies of psychology as a relatively autonomous field of scientific inquiry and as a discipline that could comport well with a Christian theological anthropology?

RA: Indeed. Each time Tom Torrance visited our campus, he was appalled at the way in which theology, psychology, and even world mission existed in their own academic ghettos, with minimal contact and interaction. He thought nearby Cal Tech offered a better model! I once confronted our former president David Hubbard in a faculty meeting with this concern, and he threw up his hands in frustration and said that it was purely a matter of pragmatism in order to have the three schools on the same campus at all. There was neither biblical nor theological basis for such separation of disciplines, he admitted, but the turf issues of each discipline militated against real integration! In my experience, this is true in many schools. Because early theological training focused almost entirely upon preparation for Christian ministry as pastors and educators, the emergence of psychological theories into pastoral care came primarily from the secular field. Attempts to "baptize" some of these theories and therapeutic practices so as to admit them into what was considered to be the domain of pastoral theology caused anxiety among many theologians and scorn from psychologists committed to the integrity of their discipline. For this reason, the concept of a Christian psychology faces a difficult task in hope of being accepted by the academic community. It really should not be that way. Einstein's approach to physics certainly carried at least a generically theistic assumption that the operation of the universe was somehow contingent upon a force or power outside the universe. The assumption that creation itself is contingent upon a Creator does not appear to violate the laws of physics, even though the Creator has no name! When theology gives a name to the Creator as the One on whom creation is contingent, it allows both physics and theology to operate with the same paradigm, even though each has its own discipline of approach, concerns, and practice. If psychology and theology are, as disciplines, each contingent upon the same paradigm that represents the objective nature of their unique concern, then integration is more of an effort at collaboration than convergence.

For all of the inadequacies of various attempts at integration, there have been many substantial contributions. I have worked with and alongside of Christian psychologists committed to integration, despite the fact that a lack of a coherent construal of human personhood allows a good deal of ambiguity and confusion. Overcoming the dualism inherent in the integration project would require first of all an epistemological shift from conventions of thought framed in the human mind to paradigmatic structures of reality emerging out of contact with the human person, the "subject who is the object" (Barth) for both psychology and theology. If the person of Jesus Christ is really the objective reality as to the nature of both God and humanity, would not the psychologist and the theologian both want to sit at his feet, and would not that make both psychology and theology Christian? What do you think?

TS: Sounds like a good starting point for a follow-up multidisciplinary project for The Society of Christian Psychology! As a Christian theologian, what do you think about the specific project of "Christian psychology" along the lines of what T. F. Torrance did in his massive epistemological work toward a convergence, not simply a collaboration, between theological and natural science? Would such a project qualify as "Christian psychology" and not merely disjunctive dialogue or compartmentalized conversation that passes for "integration"?

RA: This is an interesting suggestion. I explored this briefly in an earlier article, "Isomorphic indicators in psychological and theological science" (Anderson, 1989). I suggested that a convergence between theology and psychology can be found in their common interest in the nature of the human self as being-in-becoming. This convergence could be understood as an isomorphic structure where, despite different "ancestry," theology and psychology attempt to explain and give meaning to human experience as grounded in being (ontology), experienced in a knowing way (epistemology), and open to change by the reality of transcendent being which moves the self toward goals that offer healing and hope (teleology). Torrance (1985) has argued that our modern era has suffered a culture split where understanding (*Verstehen*) has been separated from explanation *(Erklären)* with the result that questions of meaning and values have been isolated from questions of nature and behavior. Scientific approaches, especially in the study of human behavior, have thus tended to exclude non-empirical and non-verifiable phenomena as irrelevant to the task of developing an explanatory model as a basis for personal knowledge (psychology) and as a set of standards for a healing intervention (therapy). Theology, for its part, surrendered the observable and measurable world to the scientists and technicians and took up questions of ultimate and abstract reality for its own faith in revelation, dogma, and spirituality (piety). Torrance further developed the concept of the social co-efficient of theological knowledge as an interconnection between the self and the world as a lived and experienced reality. This calls for a closer integration between the social coefficients of theological and scientific knowledge, if there is to take place fruitful and effective interchange of knowledge between the two disciplines. In order for this to happen, psychology will need to move beyond its own "Newtonian" captivity to static laws of human behavior (as did field theory physics) and allow for some aspect of contingency between predictable behavior and personal being. From the perspective of theology, says Torrance (1981), humans are clearly made the focal point in the interrelations between God and the universe, which echoes Einstein. If a "Christian psychology" can resist becoming a discipline in its own right and push both psychology and theology in the direction of exploring this "new universe" of human spirituality, it may well serve a valuable and revolutionary purpose.

I realize that by introducing the concept of "spirituality" I have opened a Pandora's' box. Forms of contemporary spirituality cross a wide spectrum, embracing outright secular and humanistic expressions of spirituality to intensely religious forms. Keith Miller (1997, p. 65) extends spirituality to the entire spectrum of our earthly life when he says, "Spirituality begins with the renewing and satisfying of the soul, and extends to every aspect of the Christian's life before God and others." Dietrich Bonhoeffer (1998, p. 62) argued that human spirituality is the core of the self as it becomes a self through social relation with others. My own definition of spirituality follows that of Bonhoeffer in that it is an essential, non-religious reach of the human self for connection to a transcendent personal being (God) as well as the intrinsic capacity for human social relations. In viewing human spirituality in this way, I feel that we can overcome the dualism that often results from contrasting a spiritual (religious) and secular (psychological) view of the human self and then attempting to produce and integrated approach.

TS: Do you think it ironic that many attempts to "integrate" theology and psychology are based on dualistic premises, giving the "upper hand," as it were, to psychology as a science or Christian faith as based on ultimate truth and then, one way or another, integrating, dialoguing, prioritizing, or compartmentalizing these presumably disparate ways of knowing? What do you think of applying T. F. Torrance's unitary way of scientific thinking, coupled with his understanding of differentiated modes of rationality, as a way forward for psychologists who want to be both Christian and scientific and have a sense of wholeness about what they're doing. Do you think his paradigm of a genuinely scientific approach to knowledge, whatever the field, pertains to and advances a deeper sense of "integration"? If so, what would you contribute as a creative conception to the project of a unitary relation between Christian psychology and theology?

RA: I use the term "integration," but view it as grounded in the very nature of human personhood. A Christian who provides counseling, whether pastoral care through the church, professional therapy in a private practice, or even an academic professor of theology(!), can and ought to have a competence that relates to the full integrative task of being and becoming human. That is the bottom line and the bigger agenda. "Troubled persons" are first of all human persons and are the primary texts for integration to be read and interpreted by the therapist or teacher in designing methods and strategies for Christian caregiving and education. In this sense, Christian psychology entails a participation in the hermeneutical task that each person must undertake in finding meaning and purpose in life, what Charles Gerkin (1984) called "the hermeneutics of the self." This demands a developed competence fully equal to the integrative task of being and becoming human on the part of the client. If all humans are spiritual beings, as I have said, as well as emotional and physical, as I think they are, then a psychologist who is not personally aware of and involved in his or her own spiritual life will lack a certain degree of competence. Thus I view integration as a multi-leveled competence on the part of a Christian caregiver or psychologist fully appropriate to the integrative task of the person seeking therapeutic relief from trauma or enablement for growth. It is a multi-leveled competence because there are at least three integrative levels in being and becoming human: psycho-somatic, psycho-social, and psycho-spiritual. In this sense, integration is not itself a discipline as a subset of psychology practiced by Christians, but what I call a coherent construal of the self as a process of seeking unity and meaning at every level. Christian psychology, I believe, offers such a coherent construal of human persons because it includes the spiritual aspect of the self without causing therapy to become religious indoctrination or confuse authentic spiritual needs with religious forms of expression. In fact, some form of translation may need to take place where the counselee presents the problem in religious language or metaphors.

TS: Given your vocation as a pastoral counselor and theologian, what do you view as the place for prayer, the Bible, or theological concepts in the counseling relationship, especially for Christians who counsel, but are not parish ministers?

RA: I am not a trained counselor or therapist, but I have done considerable pastoral counseling. My professor of pastoral counseling was trained under Carl Rogers, whose approach to clients was "non-directive" and what he called "client-centered therapy," or later, "person-centered therapy." Using this approach I was told to "do no harm" by allowing the client to actualize latent drives toward health and wholeness. This "humanistic" approach did not take into consideration what we were taught theologically about the effects of sin and the basic inability of persons to move toward healing and health without some type of transforming experience of grace. The fact is, for a beginning pastoral counselor, it worked pretty well until some of the persons who came for counseling introduced the issues of guilt, shame, sin, and need for forgiveness at a deeper level than the liturgical rituals of worship or their personal devotions resolved. I did not use the Bible in counseling except when asked by the counselee, and only later discovered the approach of "nouthetic counseling" where biblical texts were used to address what were construed as spiritual problems concealed in psychological categories. I was suspicious of this approach from the start, for many who sought help were already conflicted by the implied assumption that biblical truth could resolve their deeper spiritual and emotional struggles. In fact, some were in distress precisely because of their inability to assimilate "God's truth" into their personal lives and Christian worldviews. And yet, there is a place for using resources as therapeutic aids that relate to the spiritual dimension of a counselee's struggle for competence in working at her or his own hermeneutic task of finding meaning and purpose in life. I have often used the Bible in just such a way, as a spiritual saga and theological truth, with the focus on what the client hears or understands from the biblical text rather than what the therapist "teaches." The "hermeneutic moment" in the therapy session occurs when the client has begun the process of self-interpretation in the context of new insights. There are many resources that can contribute to this hermeneutic process, and the Bible can be one of these, provided it adds meaningfully to the insight and growth process of the counselee.

TS: Do you see a need for explicit "God talk" in Christian counseling or what is the way forward for Christian psychologists who are not merely "person-centered" or "Bible-based"?

RA: Let me give you an example. A Christian psychologist whom I will call Sue, shared with me her uneasy conscience when one of her counselees expressed appreciation for the positive outcomes of the therapy, but said, "I know that you are a Christian and so am I. I tried to change by reading the Bible and praying, but it never worked. And one thing I noticed during our counseling times, you never prayed with me or used the Bible to tell me how I should try to be more like Christ. How is it that you could help me when God couldn't?" Sue told me that her uneasy conscience resulted from the fact that she had deliberately avoided bringing religion into the counseling sessions even though she knew very well that the Bible and Christian faith are resources for emotional healing for herself, and ought then to be for others. I think that for her, integration remained stuck at the level of theory. She is quite competent in use of clinical strategies to promote personal growth and healing for her client. "God talk" has not been integrated into her therapeutic strategy at the conceptual level. She feels that this is where she needs integration in order to satisfy her conscience as to being a Christian psychologist. But if she feels uneasy or even has a twinge of guilt, it is more likely to be because she feels that she might have "failed" to integrate her own Christian faith, or even God, into her therapeutic practice. The fact that the client expressed significant integrative growth at the level of her own humanity does not register as an effect produced by the Spirit of God in the life of the client. What she may need more than a conceptual scheme of integration between psychology and Christian faith is a biblical paradigm of the human person as an integrative gestalt. She has accepted the theological dogma that human persons are created in the image of God and that saving grace through Jesus Christ restores that image. She believes that one becomes a child of God through grace alone, by faith. It is likely that her church has not helped her to see that the image of God is actually a gestalt of human selfhood experienced in healthy relationships. It is likely that her psychological training in personality theory and therapeutic techniques did not provide a paradigm of the human person as an integrative process in which the spiritual as well as the emotional constitute the gestalt of selfhood. In other words, because psychology and theology (faith) each were formed as disciplines, being a Christian psychologist carried with it ambivalence at the very core. Once she realized that she was really competent to deal with the emotional as well as spiritual needs of her client, her "psychology" moved out of being a subdiscipline of human care-giving to become a holistic psychology related to whole persons, she became a multi-dimensional therapist, not merely an integration-oriented one.

TS: Last question! Do you think a pluralistic paradigm could advance not only Christian psychology but also Christian theology?! As Karl Barth observed when he returned as an observer at Vatican II, renewal (Roman Catholic), in this example, first and foremost calls for *our* renewal (Protestant), especially those of us who call ourselves "evangelical"!

RA: Todd, I think that the problem of epistemological dualism is endemic to both theology and psychology when created reality is interpreted and explained in non-scientific terms and human conventions of thought become reified in a nominalistic form independent of the experienced reality that give rise to them. This is the kind of dualism confronted by Jesus when the law of Moses was torn out of the living organism of a redemptive community and became the "letter that kills," rather than the Spirit that gives life (2 Cor 3:6). From the Greek side, running parallel to the Hebrew, Heidegger (1959, pp. 185-186) says that Plato began the detachment of logos as the "gathering" of truth (*aletheia*) from the "truth of being" and made into a "standard of correctness." This became, of course, the basis for what in theology we call propositional revelation, truth statements that purport to be about God without really encountering him as the living Lord of truth! I suspect that psychology has its own way of making propositional statements about the human self and thus encounters the same problem of dualism. While theology and psychology each have their own form of dualism, the relation between the two has become a kind of "meta-dualism." When the camel's head of psychology crept under the tent, theology responded by driving the tent stakes deeper and forcing psychology back to its own tent. Periodically, each emerges from their secure sanctuaries of knowledge to engage in dialogue under the guise of integration. They can even produce integration journals in which they explore each other's privileged documents without yielding their private parts for examination. It was not always so. While the biblical period is considered to be a time of scientific naiveté, the astrologers of the ancient world were not invited to dialogue, but were discredited as the workers of mere human imagination cloaked in religious devotion. The biblical authors had no time for cosmic dualism. The redeemer God is also the creator God and has arranged the cosmos precisely as it is, and made it subject to his own purpose. In the days of Jesus, mental illness was not relegated to a separate sphere as an autonomous and alien force but identified, again naively, as due to unclean spirits (demons) that were subject to divine authority. Again, this was a rejection of what might be termed a psychological/theological dualism, for the same hermeneutic by which physical ailments were diagnosed and treated was used with regard to emotional and mental disorder. What was considered inhuman was treated as such under a hermeneutic of holistic humanity. A biblical view of the human person is really a "big tent" where all things are to be done "for building up"—that is, for edification. Hmm. Sounds like the title for a journal!

References

Anderson, R. S. (1975). *Historical transcendence and the reality of God*. Grand Rapids, MI: Eerdmans.

Anderson, R. S. (1986). The resurrection of Jesus as hermeneutical criterion. *TSF Bulletin, 9*, 9-15.

Anderson, R. S. (1989). Isomorphic indicators in psychological and theological science. *Journal of Psychology and Theology, 17*, 372-391.

Anderson, R. S. (2001). *The shape of practical theology*. Downers Grove, IL: InterVarsity Press.

Anderson, R. S. (2003). *Spiritual caregiving as secular*

sacrament. London: Jessica Kingsley.

Bonhoeffer, Dietrich. *Sanctorum communio: A theological study of the sociology of the church*. Minneapolis: Fortress Press, 1998.

Gerkin, C. (1984). *The living human document*. Nashville, TN: Abingdon.

Heidegger, M. (1959). *An introduction to metaphysics*. New Haven, CT: Yale University Press.

Miller, Keith (1997). *The secret life of the soul*. Nashville, TN: Broadman and Holman

Peck, M. S. (1987). *The different drum: Community making and peace*. New York: Simon and Schuster.

Torrance, T. (1975). *Theology in reconstruction*. Grand Rapids: Eerdmans.

Torrance, T. (1981). *Divine and contingent order*. Oxford: Oxford University Press.

Edification: Book Reviews

Review of Anderson (2007)

Something Old, Something New: Marriage and Family Ministry in a Postmodern Culture (plus other related old and new works by Ray Anderson)

Timothy A Sisemore, Edification Book Review Editor, Psychological Studies Institute, Chattanooga, TN.

Comment and Invitation:
Todd H. Speidell served as guest editor of this special issue of *Edification* dedicated to the work of Ray S. Anderson and thus of the following book review, which he coauthored with Cameron Lee of Fuller Seminary. Individuals interested in submitting book reviews to the journal in the future should contact the regular book review editor, Timothy Sisemore. His email address is tsisemore@psy.edu.

Featured Review

A Covenant Vision for Ministering to Contemporary Families

SOMETHING OLD, SOMETHING NEW: MARRIAGE AND FAMILY MINISTRY IN A POSTMODERN CULTURE. Ray S. Anderson. Eugene, OR: Wipf & Stock Publishers, 233 pp, $27.00. Reviewed by Cameron Lee (Fuller Theological Seminary, School of Psychology, Pasadena, CA) and Todd Speidell, (*Edification*, Guest Editor, Knoxville, TN), and examined in the context of other works by Ray Anderson.

Introduction

In the preface to his latest and twenty-fifth book, *Something Old, Something New: Marriage and Family Ministry in a Postmodern Culture*, pastoral theologian Ray Anderson (2007) reminisces about a course he co-taught with Dennis Guernsey for many years at Fuller Theological Seminary. The late Dennis Guernsey, then Director of the Marriage and Family Program at Fuller, challenged Anderson to name significant treatments of marriage and family relationships in Christian theological literature. Anderson was struck with the realization of the dearth of publications on the subject. He and Guernsey thus immediately undertook to create a course entitled *Theology of the Family*. For many years thereafter, Fuller students were treated to original and creative dialogues between the two professors. To this mix, Anderson brought his theological and pastoral expertise, with a deep indebtedness to Karl Barth and Dietrich Bonhoeffer. Guernsey brought his practical expertise as a theologically trained sociologist and family therapist. As Guernsey playfully put it, studying with Anderson was like reading the *New York Times*, while Guernsey himself was more like the funny pages.

Even in these seminal years, students didn't seem to mind and even reveled in the novelty of two such minds in creative dialogue, despite their distinct disciplines, personalities, and backgrounds. The collaboration and conversation between the two colleagues fascinated students. One professor would lecture, and the other would offer feisty and probing responses. Occasionally, they would trail off into completely uncharted territory, debating passionately, even to the point of turning their backs to the class. Diagrams would blossom *ex nihilo* in the bosom of the board, sprouting arrows and boxes and Greek and Hebrew words at a lively pace. Students learned quickly that any new diagrams to be copied had to be started in the middle of a fresh sheet of paper, lest they quickly run out of room—or even give up on trying to copy what they were witnessing!

From that collaboration grew a seminal text, *On Being Family* (*OBF*; Anderson & Guernsey, 1985), with alternating essays by Anderson and Guernsey—to some extent replicating in print the character of their classroom dialogue. The book includes chapters with provocative titles such as "Belonging is not a Matter of Choice," "Bonding without Bondage," and "Spirituality is a Domestic Skill." The title of that text is an extension of one of Anderson's (1982) earlier books, *On Being Human*, in which he outlines the social understanding of theological anthropology that under-girded *OBF*.

In *On Being Human* (*OBH*), Anderson (1982) pounces on Karl Barth's premise, "theology has become anthropology since God became man," so that psychological and ethical issues, such as human sexuality, marriage and family, abortion, and euthanasia, are intrinsically bound up with theological and pastoral perspectives in the concrete situations of human life (pp. viii-ix). Theological anthropology, Anderson argues, echoing Barth, deals with real humanity in a way that digs deeper than the "tragic" and truncated approaches of non-theological anthropologies—including philosophical, psychological, or even theistic anthropologies (p. 14). Jesus Christ, the true human as God himself as one among us, reveals and redeems true humanity, so that in him, not in Adam, we know our true selves (pp. 16ff.).

Along with *On Being Human* and *On Being Family*, Anderson (1986) wrote a theology of death and dying. One of us (TS) admittedly and impulsively suggested to Professor Anderson that he conclude this trilogy of books with the following enticing title: *On Being Dead*. Without a moment's hesitation, and with a twinkle in his eye, Ray retorted: "Well, I could make it a theological *ethics* of death and dying, and call it, *On Being Good and Dead!*"

Anderson's Integration of Theology and Ministry

The fundamental reality of life is that God assumed our humanity on our behalf to redeem it and renew it and restore it, so that we may be who we are and are becoming in Christ. Several of Anderson's publications will suffice to illustrate his life-long commitment to a genuine integration of theology and ministry on behalf of God's redemption of the whole person. His voluminous *Theological Foundations for Ministry* (Anderson, 1979), for example, contains nearly 800 pages of primary sources that flesh out his fundamental concern to have a genuinely integrated theology of ministry. He signals this from his opening chapter:

> One fundamental thesis will control this discussion—the thesis that ministry precedes and produces theology, not the reverse. It must immediately be added, however, that ministry is determined and set forth by God's own ministry of revelation and reconciliation in the world . . . Theology, thus, serves as the handmaid of ministry, proclaiming it as God's ministry and making known the eternal being of God . . . The 'practice' of ministry, then, is not only the appropriate context for doing theological thinking; it is itself intrinsically a theological activity (p. 7).

Anderson's praxis-oriented theology overcomes the typical dualism of theory and practice widely assumed by theoreticians and practitioners alike—including those who attempt to "apply" theory to practice, which assumes a divide between the two sides that must be somehow bridged by the ingenuity of the human mind, or by practical programs that theorize about *how* to be "practical"! Anderson's position as Senior Professor of Theology and Ministry at Fuller Theological Seminary is unique at a school with compartmentalized faculties of theology and ministry and separate schools of theology, psychology, and missiology—even though theologians, pastors, psychologists, missionaries, counselors, and teachers all purport to understand and help the *same person* towards wholeness and health. Further examples from Anderson's writings on a theology of ministry include *The Soul of Ministry* (1997) and *The Soul of God* (2004).

In an essay in *Whatever Happened to the Soul?* (Brown, Murphy, & Malony, 1998), Anderson (1998) questions whether modern scientific thinking (including the modern discipline of clinical psychology) has lost contact with the human soul (the Greek word *psyche*, after all, originally meant mind and soul), despite the fact that it is only humans who ponder the existence of a "soul." Anderson argues for a unitary view of the person, so that "body and soul" indicate "the whole person with both an interior and exterior life in the world" (pp. 175-177). People do not "have" souls, Anderson avers, but persons *are* souls—contrary to the widespread dualisms and monisms of the ages (p. 186) and consistent with the unitary theological anthropology of *OBH*, which proclaims that "reconciliation is the restoration of (our actual estranged and alienated) humanity" (p. 173).

Anderson's 1995 book, *Self Care*, extends and amplifies this unitary anthropology:

> The soul is the vitality of the body. While the body is necessary for the expression of the soul and is the soul in its outward form, the soul is the life of this particular body. That which affects the life of body affects the life of the soul; in the same way, without the soul as its source of life, the body has no life of its own (p. 23).

The person is not simply a "personality" amenable to empirical psychological observation, but a personal being created and loved by the very being of God in his own image and—in agreement with Karl Barth and T. F. Torrance— like God himself, knowable in a genuinely and deeply scientific, objective, and personal way (Anderson, 2002b, pp. 146ff.).

Lest an unwary reader think that an integrated anthropology suggests an isolated individuality, Anderson quotes the Scottish philosopher John Macmurray to underscore the social nature of a unitary and holistic anthropology:

I need you to be myself. This need is for a fully positive personal relation in which, because we trust one another, we can think and feel and act together. Only in such a relation can we really be ourselves. If we quarrel, each of us withdraws from the other into himself, and the trust is replaced by fear . . . But we will remain isolated individuals, and the cooperation between us, though it may appear to satisfy our need of one another, will not really satisfy us. For what we really need is to care for one another, and we are only caring for ourselves. We have achieved society, but not community. We have become associates, but not friends (pp. 27ff).

Thus, from the standpoint of a biblically-based social and relational anthropology, the construct of *self-esteem* should not suggest the quest for self-gratification or self-aggrandizement, but a spiritual practice of personal agency as fundamentally and essentially constituted by relation to others (pp. 102-107).

Spiritual Caregiving as Secular Sacrament (Anderson, 2003) expands and deepens one of Anderson's paradigmatic points: *all* people, whether affiliating with the supposedly "sacred" or "secular" spheres of life, are embodied social-relational beings with basic spiritual longings. "Spirituality"—not to be confused with the vague and popular neo-Gnostic parlance of our present age and particular culture—is essential to psychological health and human wholeness. Christian theological language and religious practice give explicit and overt expression to the Spirit of God in, by, and through Christ as the healing agent of humanity for wholeness and holiness in relation to self, others, and God. As Anderson asserts, the

> breach between the disciplines of theology and psychology has its roots in the failure of theology to have a biblical view of God and a failure to construct an integrative model of the human self . . . One cannot move toward health and holiness at the physical/mental level while the self is fragmented at the psycho-spiritual level (pp. 13, 77).

Christians Who Counsel (Anderson, 1990) continues this unitary view of spiritual care by arguing that fellow suffering human beings may grow together in God's grace by accepting his healing words, acts, and presence in their lives and ministries (pp. 16ff., 26). *The Shape of Practical Theology* (Anderson, 2001) is replete with case studies that illumine the nature of what Anderson calls "theological praxis," including discussions of forgiveness, clergy burnout, homosexuality, and Christian ministry to families in a postmodern society. These themes nicely frame our consideration of his latest book on marriage and family ministry.

A Theological Vision for Family Ministry

Something Old, Something New (*SOSN*; Anderson, 2007) is clearly a continuation of Ray Anderson's creative process of uniting theology and ministry. Although Anderson's theological vision has remained steadfast, the social institution of the family itself has continued to change in the two decades since *OBF* was published. As the title of chapter 8 of *SOSN* announces: "Families are not what they used to be!" What the book represents, therefore, is the creative reflection of a mature theologian on contemporary issues facing American families in a postmodern age.

Families themselves, however, are not the primary audience for this book. Anderson writes with two complementary voices: the pastor and the theologian. Some of the book reads as if addressed more directly to families. Many of these sections are topical additions to the more theoretically-oriented work in *OBF*. For example, in a chapter entitled, "When Those Who Love You Hurt You," Anderson deals with the issue of family violence. There he argues that abuse distorts a person's self- evaluation, and offers the metaphor of the need for vision correction. He writes:

> When we have been the victim of abuse we need to go to specialists in non-abusive love and care. More than that, we need to ask them to conduct an eye examination by asking us what we see when we take a good look at ourselves. We need to trust their vision in order to correct our own (Anderson, 2007, p. 117).

One can imagine a pastor saying something like this to a counselee. Pastorally written passages like this one could be of direct benefit to individuals struggling with abusive family histories.

Other passages, however, assume a much higher level of theological and philosophical sophistication in the reader, particularly in the chapters that are more devoted to establishing the book's theological perspective. The opening two chapters, for example, briefly trace the emergence of a postmodern perspective and its relationship to a contemporary understanding of morality. Here we find sentences such as the following:

> What the metaphysical version of reality seeks to establish by appealing to impersonal concepts of the good, a theological view of reality finds moral stability and certainty in the character of God as Creator. Instead of abstracting away from the created world

to find the moral absolute as a formal principle, the biblical tradition finds the moral absolute in God's word of creation and redemption (Anderson, 2007, p. 16).

Passages like these, written in the theologian's voice, point to the essential place that a doctrine of covenant should have in a theology of family, which Anderson unfolds in subsequent chapters. They are written mainly for the edification of family ministers. Anderson's goal is not to prescribe step-by-step ministry strategies based on some general construct such as "the postmodern family," but to help those who minister to families to achieve a deeper vision of the *telos* of family life. In Anderson's view, this would be the theological precondition of their work.

The early chapters of the book set forth the postmodern problematic. Christian theologians have begun to realize that "their construct of a biblical version of the family was essentially a reflection of . . . the 'modern' period of western intellectual and ethical thought, baptized as the Christian norm" (Anderson, 2007, p. 3). In this vein, Anderson suggests areas of agreement with a postmodern worldview. For example, Christians may rightly reject the modernist myth of purely objective knowledge, recognizing how our perceptions of what is true are shaped by participation in community. This has implications, of course, for our understanding of the church:

> The distrust of reason as the sole basis for truth means that truth must be experienced to be believed, and it is in the church as the community of believers that the truth of the gospel is experienced and lived out (p. 3).

We may also appreciate the postmodern emphasis on narrative as a vehicle of meaning. Here we are reminded of Hauerwas' (1981) notion of the "story-formed community," where the life of the church itself constitutes a social ethic.

At the same time, however, the condition of postmodernity is characterized by social instability and the bifurcation of belief from lived values. As Anderson (2007) observes:

> [I]n North America, up to 90% of the population will express some kind of belief in God or a divine being to whom they look for guidance and help. At the same time, these people can be observed spending their time and money on things that bring immediate gratification rather than long-term fulfillment. The majority of people believe that marriage should be a lifelong commitment, and yet, more than half of all marriages fail due to a perceived loss of personal value in the relationship. As a result, the basic moral structure of our social institutions of family and community appears to be falling apart (pp. 11-12).

The underlying difficulty is not merely one of behavior but more so of moral vision. Moreover, if an inadequate moral vision leads to the weakening of family life, the converse is also true, because it is in families that such vision is shaped:

> When the Bible speaks of character, it does so in terms of core human moral and spiritual values, rather than religious rituals and regulations. The critical moral experiences that contribute to the formation of character do not take place in the church, but in the family and in the daily lives of people in their primary relationships (p. 18).

In a sense, family is both producer and product of a culture's value socialization, which is why it is crucial for family ministers to consider the moral vision within which they operate.

Different moral orders are socially constructed on the basis of competing visions of the source of moral authority. Such orders can be based on naturalistic assumptions, socio-cultural conventions, or even interpersonal contracts, but which of these is a sufficient basis for grappling with the moral demands of family life? Which rationale would help us to explain what family members owe to one another, and why?

Recognizing competing versions of reality, each with its own vision of moral order, Anderson (2007) proposes his own: the "*redemptive order*, where the moral order is personal and covenantal" (p. 21, italics in original). He writes:

> The biblical concept of covenant makes all other orders contingent upon the love and purpose of God as the source of moral authority. The natural, conventional and interpersonal orders each have their own moral order and forms of moral authority . . . contingent upon the moral authority of divine covenant love. Covenant order is not merely interpersonal, based upon the assumption that each person is a free moral agent, but it is personal and intimate, so that the character of the relationship as an embodiment of love creates a form of moral empowerment to love in return (p. 21).

A covenantal understanding provides a transcendent framework for the loyalty and commitment that sustain the theological praxis of family life.

Subsequent chapters develop the covenantal theme more thoroughly. Anderson (2007) begins with theological anthropology. We are God's creatures, sharing certain characteristics with non-human creatures, but what makes us specifically human originates from outside our creatureliness. Anderson interprets the Genesis account of the creation of humanity as male and female to suggest that humans, created in God's image, are intrinsically social. (As described earlier, a more extended treatment can be found in *OBH*; Anderson, 1982.) What it means to be a person, and not merely a creature, is to exist in personal relationships, implying an openness to other persons as itself the spiritual dimension of our existence.

A theological understanding of parenting, in particular, consists of much more than the mere creaturely process of biological reproduction. Though the God-given responsibility can be fulfilled by other adults, it is normally a child's parent who "summons the latent mystery of the 'I' into relation, which is a summons into responsibility, into communion" (Anderson, 2007, p. 30). Thus the development of personhood begins in childhood, in the context of the relationship to one's parents. Understood within the context of a transcendent covenantal vision, parenthood is "accountability to the command of God" in which parents "stand in a relation to their children in a way analogous to the way in which God is related to his people, as Father" (pp. 30, 31). The role of parents, therefore, is to call forth the personhood of their children in such a way as to usher them into the biblical metanarrative that provides them with the basis for character and moral identity.

From the standpoint of secular psychology, a relational anthropology in itself is unremarkable. Various psychological theories already recognize the intrinsic sociality of human existence and development. Psychoanalytic object relations theorists like Ronald Fairbairn have long taught that relatedness to a significant human other is a primary human drive, in contrast with the classical Freudian notion of the gratification of individual desire. Recent treatments of neuroscientific research point in the same direction (e.g. Goleman, 2006). Brothers (1997), for example, writes:

> In contrast to contemporary cognitive neuroscience, which views the mind as a kind of closet . . . I take mind to be irreducibly transactional. Rather than something packed inside a solitary skull, it is a dynamic entity defined by transactions with the rest of the world . . . [T]he essence of thought is not its isolated neural basis, but its social use. (p. 146)

Even our creatureliness, it would seem, entails a neurophysiology that is hard-wired for sociality. Thus, human development is not the mere unfolding of innate individual potential but is fundamentally and intrinsically social.

Anderson's contribution based on Barth, Bonhoeffer, Macmurray, and others does not intend to grant theological credence to the insights of psychological theory and research, although he argues for a teleological understanding of family that cannot be derived from an understanding of our creatureliness. His social theory of personhood puts forth that "existence in community (as co-humanity) is actually and logically prior to existence as a discrete individual. The biblical concept of covenant gives historical meaning to this fundamental order of humanity" (Anderson, 2007, p. 155). God's covenant love is the paradigm; covenant is the "teleological goal of family" (p. 45).

> The telos of family is the realization of covenant love . . . Belonging is a gift, not an achievement. The *quintessence* of family, thus, is this shalom of covenant love (p. 47).

Again, covenantal love is quintessential for the parent-child relationship, through which the developing child is socialized into authentic personhood. (Professor Anderson is quite fond of the word "quintessential" [and it's an in-joke among his students]. One day in class, he was searching for an apt illustration for his concept of humanity as cohumanity, noting that humans were created with two eyes, ears, arms, and legs. "Two of everything!" he announced triumphantly. Students began to snicker, and he quickly recognized his faux pas. "Well," he admitted sheepishly, "not two of everything." But then he brightened. "After all," he said, jabbing the air with his finger, "some things are quintessential!")

Marriage, too, is a covenant partnership. Here, promise-making and promise-keeping are central: "The greatest threat to the family for the future is not poor marriages, or conflicted family structures, but loss of belief in the making of promise" (Anderson, 2007, p. 66). Coincidentally, in the years since the publication of *OBF*, state legislatures have begun to enact "covenant marriage" policies in which those intending to wed voluntarily submit to legally binding agreements that make it more difficult to dissolve the marriage in the future. Such a decision on the part of a couple is an attempt to take promise seriously.

Even with the adoption of such language, so-called "covenant" marriage is still a contractual agreement, backed by the legislative authority of the state. One might say that the contractual promise helps hold the marriage together. But what holds the promise? To say that God's covenant love is the telos of family does not simply mean that families stand or fall upon the promises family members make to one another. It means that the divine covenant is itself a resource when human promises fail, precisely through providing the telos that mere promise-making might lack:

> From the human perspective, the essence of a marriage is the social contract explicitly grounded in a relationship of human sexuality, male and female, which finds its implicit source of covenant love in God's own commandment and gift of love. In this sense, marriage is not a product of each individual's effort, but rather a mutual task. A shared task or purpose is what orients a marriage relationship to the future, and causes it to endure (Anderson, 2007, p. 71).

Anderson does not idealize the idea of covenant marriage. On the horizontal plane, marriage is still a frangible social contract, yet the vertical dimension of divine covenant may still be expressed through such contracts, providing the transcendent purpose that marriage needs.

Recent treatments of covenant marriage written expressly for couples provide parallels. Chapman (2003), for example, rightly insists that "the Christian's ultimate call is not the call to develop a good marriage; the Christian's call is to be a disciple of Jesus Christ" (p. 4). Covenant is a biblical alternative to secular understandings of marriage based on contractual agreements. With Anderson, Chapman rightly recognizes that marriage is in fact a social contract but not *merely* a contract. The usual Old Testament heroes serve as examples of God's covenant initiative—Noah, Abraham, Moses, David—though Chapman does not distinguish the unilateral promise of the Abrahamic covenant from the conditional blessings of the Mosaic covenant (e.g., Horton, 2006; Lowery, 2002). Chapman describes covenant marriage as characterized by unconditional promise, steadfast love, and permanent commitment.

There is a tendency in Chapman's (2003) and similar works to distill the biblical teaching on covenant into an abstract list of bulleted principles. It is unclear whether covenant is applied to marriage analogically or if there is a more substantive connection with the divine covenant that could be explicated theologically. To be fair, this latter connection is not always concretely clear in Anderson (2007) either. A challenge for the future would be to detail more closely in what ways God's covenant love is a source of marital love and commitment in a way that ordinary couples themselves could understand.

Whereas Chapman's (2003) book quickly takes a therapeutic turn, Anderson (2007) demonstrates a larger ecclesiological vision that Chapman lacks.

In Anderson's ecclesiology, family ministry is not conceived as a professional sub-specialization in the manner of therapy. To borrow a phrase from Walter Brueggemann (1993), the church's ministry of spiritual formation is "coherent construal," or the ability "to perceive, embrace, and enact the world according to the peculiar memory and vision of faith held by the gospel community" (p. 98)—and that memory and vision is of the history and anticipation of God's covenant love. The practical question is whether a teleological and covenantal perspective such as Anderson describes can be maintained by families in isolation or by well-meaning Christian individuals who are unwittingly holding themselves to human striving for perfect standards of a "Christian marriage." It is not about the removal of difficulties in Christian families. Rather, it is but one manifestation of the church's larger commitment to the spiritual formation of its members.

The church *does* ministry because it *is* itself the covenant community of God (cf. also Grenz, 1994). In Dennis Guernsey's (1983, 1985) phrase, the church is therefore a "family of families," which does not mean that it is the church's task simply to reproduce family-like affective relationships at a larger level. Modern companionate conceptions of family relationships (and their exaggerated postmodern cousins) should not drive an ecclesiology of family life and ministry. Rather, the reverse is true: authentic covenant community creates parity for all believers—regardless of their family status (those who are married with children do not have a privileged status)—and parity provides the proper context for redeeming family disorder for all of the church community's members.

> In this way we see that the original order of the family is grounded in the new family of God, and that the moral authority that upholds the order of the family as a social institution is grounded in the spiritual authority of love as expressed through Jesus Christ and as experienced in Christian community. The church, then, as the new family of God, demonstrates the authority of Scripture by renewing marriage and family where it has fallen into disorder, and by recreating marriage and family where it has been destroyed (Anderson, 2007, p. 96).

Therapeutic applications of covenant principles of relationship can be useful but ultimately need to be located within a community that itself embodies covenant.

In a postmodern context, this redemptive ministry cannot consist of the imposition of proof-texts to enforce conformity to supposedly biblical norms of family life. Anderson (2007) reminds us, for example, that

> Jesus was crucified on exegetical grounds . . . Tearing the biblical text out of the womb of covenantal love and mercy, they used it to nail truth to the cross. In the name of biblical authority, some define morality in terms of traditional forms of marriage and family; they have forgotten God's moral judgment against the formal principle of the law when used to sanction loveless and lifeless formality (p. 89).

The church as "story-formed community" (Hauerwas, 1981) is the custodian not of immutable moral rules, but the story of covenant love that supplies the creative telos of family life as the theological core of family ministry in a postmodern age of shifting norms:

> For the church, not only must be a "family of families" . . . but also a positive force in creating and supporting healthy families. In this way, the church must also become active in the reinventing of family in the postmodern culture and contribute to the discussion of what constitutes 'familying' in the midst of changing forms of family life. The question facing us is not whether or not the concept of family is becoming obsolete but whether the kind of family we experience leads us to be more or less human (Anderson, 2007, p. 203).

Anderson's latest work surpasses *OBF* in providing a more coherently covenantal vision for family ministry. Such a ministry substitutes an ethos of caring for curing, and freeing for fixing; the imposition of moral imperatives gives way to empowering families spiritually (Anderson, 2007, pp. 85-89). Anderson creatively applies his teleological and covenantal perspective to a variety of contemporary concerns, including abuse and family violence (chapter 9), divorce and remarriage (chapter 10), homosexuality (chapter 11), the meaning of human life in the face of death (chapter 12), and grand-parenting (chapter 15).

In these chapters, however, the covenantal perspective is usually more implicit than explicit. Chapter 10, for example, is entitled "Bonding without Bondage" as an extension of the chapter on divorce that appeared earlier in *OBF* (Anderson, 1985). The central theme of this chapter is the divine command rather than covenant. Anderson (2007) understands the command of God as "a summons to think, act, and live so as to be accountable to God himself" (p. 119), as opposed to some more abstract form of biblical rules or regulations. This means that marriage itself may be a calling, but cannot be equated with a command:

> The command of God under-girds temporal life and calls us to responsibility in our present situation. If one undertakes marriage as a calling of God for one's life, it stands under the command of God. If one remains single as a responsible life within the context of cohumanity, this life too stands under the command of God. That is, neither marriage nor celibacy can be absolutely equated with the command of God in such a way that one or the other has a higher status. (p. 120)

Marriage as a calling is indissoluble because it stands under the command, not because it is itself commanded, or as Anderson puts it, "marriage is a possibility, not a necessity" (p. 122), which leaves open the theological possibility that the sovereignty of God includes his freedom to "declare . . . that a marriage is a non-marriage" (p. 123). Anderson returns here to the concept of covenant, asking what God's judgment might mean on a marriage that has not exhibited any marks of being a covenant partnership. This position provides a helpful theological alternative to a rule of indissolubility, on the one hand, or the absolute freedom to dissolve the relationship on the basis of emotional criteria, on the other, but Anderson's treatment of the divine command could be more thoroughly and explicitly tied to the covenant theme that pervades the rest of the book.

Overall, the title *Something Old, Something New* aptly describes the book itself. The work is the culmination of decades of theological reflection on ministry and family life. Those who have read Anderson's previous work will find much that is familiar here. At the same time, they will also find fresh reflections for our contemporary situation. Family ministers in particular will be challenged to develop a more holistic covenant vision for their work, a vision which will need to be translated into the day-to-day language of the congregation, nudging believers toward a shared understanding of the church as the covenant people of God. To that end, we would recommend supplemental reading, including Grenz's (1994) treatment of the church as an eschatological covenant community or Gushee's (2004) contribution to the marriage education movement, which draws upon themes of covenant and kingdom.

As in the seminary course from which this work originated, charts and diagrams abound, but their implications are not always fully nor systematically explicated. Indeed, some chapters, pregnant with ideas, are worthy of book-length treatment in their own right. All of this means that the book leaves the conversation open for further reflection and dialogue. For those who minister to families and desire grist for the theological mill, it is a conversation worth engaging.

References

Anderson, R. S. (Ed.) (1979). *Theological foundations for ministry: Selected readings for a theology of the church in ministry.* Grand Rapids, MI: Eerdmans.

Anderson, R. S. (1982). *On being human: Essays in theological anthropology.* Grand Rapids, MI: Eerdmans.

Anderson, R. S. (1986). *Theology, death and dying.* Oxford: Blackwell.

Anderson, R. S. (1990). *Christians who counsel: The vocation of wholistic therapy.* Grand Rapids, MI: Zondervan.

Anderson, R. S. (1995). *Self care: A theology of personal empowerment and spiritual healing.* Wheaton, IL: Bridgepoint.

Anderson, R. S. (1997). *The soul of ministry: Forming leaders for God's people.* Louisville, KY: Westminster/John Knox.

Anderson, R. S. (1998). On being human: The spiritual saga of a creaturely soul. In W. S. Brown, N. Murphy, & H. N. Malony (Eds.), *Whatever happened to the soul?* (pp 175-194). Minneapolis, MN: Augsburg Fortress.

Anderson, R. S. (2001). *The shape of practical theology: Empowering ministry with theological praxis.* Downers Grove, IL: InterVarsity.

Anderson, R. S. (2002a). The epistemological relevance of laughter. In T. Speidell (Ed.), *On being Christian . . . and human: Essays in celebration of Ray S. Anderson.* Eugene, OR: Wipf and Stock.

Anderson, R. S. (2002b). The social ecology of human personhood: Implications of Dietrich Bonhoeffer's theology for psychology. In T. Speidell (Ed.), *On being a person: A multidisciplinary approach to personality theories.* Eugene, OR: Cascade.

Anderson, R. S. (2003). *Spiritual caregiving as secular sacrament: A practical theology for professional caregivers.* New York: John Knox.

Anderson, R. S. (2004). *The soul of God: A theological memoir.* Eugene, OR: Wipf and Stock.

Anderson, R. S. (2007). *Something old, something new: Marriage and family ministry in a postmodern culture.* Eugene, OR: Wipf and Stock.

Anderson, R. S., & Guernsey, D. B. (1985). *On being family: A social theology of the family.* Grand Rapids, MI: Eerdmans.

Bonhoeffer, D. (1963). *Communion of saints.* New York: Harper and Row.

Brothers, L. (1997). *Friday's footprint: How society shapes the human mind.* New York: Oxford.

Brown, W. S., Murphy, N., & Malony, H. N. (Eds.) (1998). *Whatever happened to the soul?* Minneapolis, MN: Augsburg Fortress.

Brueggemann, W. (1993). *Biblical perspectives on evangelism.* Nashville: Abingdon.

Chapman, G. D. (2003). *Covenant marriage.* Nashville, TN: B & H Publishing.

Goleman, D. (2006). *Social intelligence.* New York: Bantam.

Grenz, S. J. (1994). *Theology for the community of God.* Nashville, TN: Broadman & Holman.

Guernsey, D. B. (1983). *A new design for family ministry.* Elgin, IL: David C. Cook.

Guernsey, D. B. (1985). What kind of family is the church? In R. S. Anderson & D. B. Guernsey, *On being family: A social theology of the family* (pp. 155-159). Grand Rapids, MI: Eerdmans.

Gushee, D. P. (2004). *Getting marriage right.* Grand Rapids, MI: Baker.

Hauerwas, S. (1981). *A community of character.* Notre Dame, IN: University of Notre Dame Press.

Horton, M. (2006). *God of promise.* Grand Rapids, MI: Baker.

Lowery, F. (2002). *Covenant marriage: Staying together for life.* West Monroe, LA: Howard.

www.ingramcontent.com/pod-product-compliance
Lightning Source LLC
Chambersburg PA
CBHW080448110426
42743CB00016B/3321